Gross Motor Fun

A Collection of Developmentally Age-Appropriate Gross Motor Activities Designed to Improve Classroom Performance

by
Michael C. Abraham C.A.P.E.

illustrated by
Vanessa Countryman

Publisher
Key Education Publishing Company, LLC
Minneapolis, Minnesota

◆▼●■★◆▼●■★◆▼●■★◆▼●■★◆▼●■★◆▼●■★◆▼●■★◆▼●■★◆▼●■★◆▼●■★◆▼

CONGRATULATIONS ON YOUR PURCHASE OF A KEY EDUCATION PRODUCT!

The editors at Key Education are former teachers who bring experience, enthusiasm, and quality to each and every product. Thousands of teachers have looked to the staff at Key Education for new and innovative resources to make their work more enjoyable and rewarding. Key Education is committed to developing and publishing educational materials that will assist teachers in building a strong and developmentally appropriate curriculum for young children.

PLAN FOR GREAT TEACHING EXPERIENCES WHEN YOU USE EDUCATIONAL MATERIALS FROM KEY EDUCATION PUBLISHING COMPANY, LLC

◆▼●■★◆▼●■★◆▼●■★◆▼●■★◆▼●■★◆▼●■★◆▼●■★◆▼●■★◆▼●■★◆▼●■★◆▼●■★◆▼

Credits
Author: Michael Abraham
Publisher: Sherrill B. Flora
Creative Director: Annette Hollister-Papp
Illustrations: Vanessa Countryman
Cover Design: Annette Hollister-Papp
Editors: Karen Seberg, Claude Chalk
Production: Key Education Production Staff

Key Education welcomes manuscripts and product ideas from teachers. For a copy of our submission guidelines, please send a self-addressed, stamped envelope to:

Key Education Publishing Company, LLC
Acquisitions Department
9601 Newton Avenue South
Minneapolis, Minnesota 55431

About the Author

Michael C. Abraham, C.A.P.E., has been working closely together with children with special needs for 31 years. An honor graduate from Springfield College, with numerous advanced degrees from Southern Connecticut State University and Fairfield University, Mike Abraham has served the Fairfield Public Schools and it's children for the past 31 years. As a nationally recognized Certified Adapted Physical Educator, his mission has always been a "kids come first" approach in their education. Working closely with educators, Mike has provided numerous professional development workshops assisting and supporting teachers as they attempt to educate children with special needs within the general education program. Whether working in the aquatic program providing therapeutic techniques to assist physically challenged children, or working closely with general education classroom teachers demonstrating how children with fine motor and sensory integration difficulties can access the curriculum, Mike has brought his expertise in all endeavours with the child's best interest first. In addition to his "regular" responsibilities Mike has also served as the district instructor, assisting teachers with strategies and techniques to manage student behaviors when they escalate with a aggressive verbal and/or physical component. Mike has published various books and articles in the areas of Special Education, Adapted Physical Education, Movement and Music and Sensory Integration.

Dedication

To my dedicated and loyal past and present colleagues of the Fairfield Public Schools in the Physical Education Department. Under the leadership of David T. Abraham, Coordinator of Physical Education, these professionals have worked very closely with all students meeting their needs and modifying and adapting curriculum. "Children come first" and these professionals have adopted that theme as they have engaged their students. It has been my pleasure to work closely with these professionals.

Standard Book Number: 978-1-602680-03-8 *Gross Motor Fun*
Copyright © 2008 by Key Education Publishing Company, LLC
Minneapolis, Minnesota 55431

Special Note

Before completing any balloon activity, ask families about latex allergies. Also, remember that uninflated or popped balloons may present a choking hazard.

◆▼●■★◆▼●■★◆▼●■★◆▼●■★◆▼●■★◆▼●■★◆▼●■★◆▼●■★◆▼●■★◆▼●■★◆▼

Contents

Preface

Educators today face numerous challenges as the umbrella of "No Child Left Behind" impacts the classroom environment and learning climate. What once may have been an experiential classroom, has become much more specific in its delivery of the curriculum, providing information that will enable students to test well. We have created classrooms in which we may be educating today's children only from the neck up. With this approach, we may have missed providing a foundation for learning that includes the concept of body-mind-spirit.

Children cannot be broken into parts. It is still the whole child we need to educate even as the academic/cognitive piece is addressed through curriculum demands. What we may miss when we engage students in the three Rs is nurturing their spirits, self-images, and self-esteems as they navigate through their educational journeys. We have many times overlooked how the body needs to be cultivated. Numerous studies and research have indicated how movement and learning are connected and that students succeed when their bodies are activated in the educational process. *Gross Motor Fun* will provide you with the tools and techniques to not only engage students with the concepts of the three Rs but also address the development of their self-images and motoric abilities (gross and fine).

Introduction

Movement is a natural part of being a child. Movement experiences should not be regularly scheduled and then disregarded; rather, movement experiences should be spontaneous in the classroom and integrated throughout the school day. Motor skill acquisition is the direct result of experience and practice. Without early opportunities to engage in active learning, many children, particularly children with special needs, begin school with inadequate motor skill development, and they do not acquire these motor skills through "natural" experiences later on in life. In addition, young children, as well as children with special needs, can learn through their movements and play—through being active. Activity lays the foundation for essential learning skills, which, in turn, affect a child's ability to read, write, and think.

Movement programs are vital, not only for the improvement of health-related fitness and motor skill development, but also for the development and enhancement of self-esteem and self-confidence, thereby enriching the psychological well-being of students. Early movement experiences have the potential to greatly enhance a child's self-image because movement experiences are so personal and because success depends so much on one's own skills and abilities. For this reason, it is critical that teachers, paraprofessionals, and parents provide positive reinforcement, and lots of it, when children attempt movement activities.

Movement programs can also provide students with vital recreational experiences. Programs assist students to use their leisure time in a satisfying and constructive manner, thereby opening doors for their fuller participation in society as adults.

Movement activities engage the whole body and address developmental concepts of laterality and directionality. Incorporating movement on opposite sides of the body, such as crawling, hand over hand climbing, and moving on a balance beam and/or outdoor playground equipment, stimulates the above concepts and has strong impact on reading and writing skills.

Gross motor skills develop before fine motor skills, and teachers need to work on strengthening the upper body and core before they can expect the hands and fingers to be well coordinated. The amount of time children are required to sit at their desks or tables emphasizes the need for gross motor development even more.

Children learn from the concrete to the abstract, and the body provides the most concrete experience available for motor planning and organization. Exploring movement creates an arena for the child to learn new ways to move and then to integrate those movements into a planned motor act. Moving freely with little structure from verbal cues and environmental restrictions, children need to be able to control their bodies in space before they can organize words and numbers on a page. The body in space movements of young children are critical for providing a base and foundation for future deskwork.

Movement experiences, as indicated through studies and research, have an impact on the social and emotional development of young children. When engaged in developmentally-appropriate gross motor activities, children succeed; this success fosters the social and emotional makeup needed for human development.

Movement and Learning

It is generally understood and accepted that physical activity can impact not only a child's physical development, but also the child's social and emotional development. Often, however, no connection is made to how physical activity can enhance a child's cognitive development. Educators need to understand the link between physical activity and learning. Here are some facts supported by numerous studies and research:

Athletics and Learning:

- As a group, students who participate in interscholastic athletics tend to perform better academically (GPA) than students who do not participate.
- Athletes in general tend to perform better academically during their sports' seasons.
- Athletes who participate in two or three sports tend to perform better academically than athletes who participate in only one sport.

Physical Activity's Effect on the Brain:

- The cerebellum (the part of the brain that processes movement) has clear pathways to the parts of the brain involved in memory, attention, spatial perception, language, complex emotional behavior, and decision making.
- Exercise increases both the number of connections among the brain's neurons and the number of capillaries around them.
- Exercise triggers the release of natural chemicals that boost the ability of neurons to communicate with each other, thus enhancing cognition.
- Exercise also triggers the release of natural chemicals that stimulate the brain's pleasure centers thereby decreasing stress, increasing self-esteem, enhancing a sense of purpose in life, and improving attitude in school.
- Vigorous aerobic exercise improves short-term memory, reaction time, and creativity.
- Children engaged in daily physical education or athletics show superior motor fitness, academic performance, and attitudes toward school when compared to their counterparts who do not participate.

The Physical Activity and Cognitive Development Connection:

- One Canadian study showed academic scores went up when one-third of the school day was devoted to physical education.
- Another Canadian study demonstrated that children who participated in five hours of vigorous physical activity a week had stronger academic performances in math, English, natural sciences, and French than did children with only two hours of physical activity per week.
- A study of third-grade children participating in dance activities showed an improvement in their reading skills of 13 percent over six months, while their peers, who were sedentary, showed a decrease of 2 percent.
- In France, children who spent eight hours a week in physical education demonstrated better academic performance, greater independence, and more maturity than students with only 40 minutes of PE a week.
- A study conducted by neurophysiologist Carla Hannaford determined that children who spent an hour a day exercising did better on exams than students who didn't exercise.
- Recent research demonstrates a direct link between fitness and intelligence, particularly in children under 16 and in the elderly.

Young Children Learn Best When Doing

Experiencing movement through the senses enhances the sensory-motor skills necessary for children to perform in the classroom. Physical activity allows children to develop their tactile, vestibular, kinesthetic/proprioceptive, and equilibrium systems. The development through physical activity of sensory systems, especially the tactile, is of primary importance for development of motor planning. In turn, motor-planning skills allow a child to organize, plan, and then execute new or unpracticed tasks.

We all know children develop at different rates. There are usually several children in each class who, for one reason or another, do not perform in the "normal" range when participating in classroom activities. Some children who have near-average or above-average intelligence perform motor tasks well below what is considered normal. Increasingly, research indicates a strong, positive relationship between a child's ability to execute perceptual-motor tasks, achieve academically, and be socially accepted by peers. Strengthening a child's motor skill development will also help that child improve academically and socially. Unfortunately, in our society, technology is partially responsible for having created an overall lack of movement in daily routines—the "couch potato" syndrome. Many children are deprived of essential motor experiences necessary for gross motor development.

When children are given opportunities to move, a "movement vocabulary" develops, integrating movement with learning. For example, the performance of action words builds greater levels of cognition as children move to these words, enhancing the concept of learning by doing. Retention of the words is improved as they are motorically imprinted in the brain. This type of active involvement demonstrates the critical connection between doing and learning.

Definitions

The following terms can assist in the development of a "motor vocabulary" as students engage in physical activities.

active listening: .... in conversation or interview, attending carefully to what is said by the other person; an awareness of both verbal and nonverbal communication

adaptive behavior: .... the manner with which the individual deals with the cultural, social, physical, and mental demands of the environment

adaptive skills: .... learned patterns of behavior, which enable individuals to fulfill their own needs and the needs of others

agility: .... ability to move the body or any of its parts in any direction quickly, easily, and with control

agnosia: .... inability to recognize a common object through one or more of the senses

agonist: .... muscles directly engaged in contraction, creating the force of movement, as distinguished from the muscles (antagonists) that relax and lengthen during the same movement

akinesia: .... motor dysfunction with resultant loss of movement

antagonist: .... muscles that, by relaxing during a movement, oppose or resist the action of the contracting muscles (agonists)

aphasia: .... inability to understand spoken words due to cerebral dysfunction

apraxia: .... inability to carry out plans to perform a complex coordinated movement

association: .... the organized process of relating the sensory information to the motor act; also, relating present and past experiences to each other

ataxia: .... inability to coordinate voluntary muscle movements, particularly those used in reaching and walking

athetotic movement: .... writhing, involuntary, irregular, arrhythmical gross movement

attention: .... concentrated direction of the mind—the engagement in the perceptual, cognitive and motor activities associated with performing skills

balance: .... ability to assume and maintain any body position against the force of gravity

body awareness: .... knowledge of the way the body parts move, for example, to turn, twist, and stretch

body image: .... perception of the body as derived from external and internal sensations

body scheme: .... automatic adjustment of skeletal parts and the tensing and relaxing of muscles necessary to maintain a position

cardiorespiratory endurance: ability of the heart and lungs to maintain efficient function during and after vigorous activity

cerebral dominance: .... tendency of one side of the brain to be more developed than the other (for example, right-handedness is controlled by the left hemisphere of the brain)

closed motor skill: .... a skill that is performed in a stable or predictable environment

cocontraction: .... simultaneous contraction of the agonist and antagonist muscles to provide stability

continuous motor skill: .... a motor skill such as swimming that requires the individual to repeatedly use the same movements

contracture: .... permanent muscular contraction in which the antagonists are paralyzed resulting from tonic spasm or loss of muscular equilibrium

coordination: .... harmonious working together of several muscles or muscle groups in the execution of complicated movements to accomplish the goal of the skill; higher coordination achieves more complex movements

developmental delay: .... maturational lag with retardation occurring in one or more of the basic domains

directionality: .... awareness of space outside of the body involving; (1) knowledge of directions in relation to right and left, in and out, and up and down; (2) the projection of one's self in space; and (3) the judging of distances between objects

discrete motor skill: .... a skill that has a definite beginning and end, such as turning on a stove, threading a needle, etc.

dynamic balance: .... ability to maintain a position while the individual is moving or the surface is moving

dyspraxia: .... difficulty in performing a motor act

equilibrium: .... state of balance or equality between opposing forces; bodily stability or balance

eye-foot coordination: .... ability to use eyes and feet together to accomplish a task

eye-hand coordination: .... ability to use eyes and hands together to accomplish a task

figure-ground discrimination: distinguishing objects or important information from the surrounding environment

fine motor coordination: .... development of the muscles to the degree that they perform specific small movements

fine motor skills: .... the binary opposite of gross motor skills requiring greater control of the small muscles and greater precision, for example, with handwriting, typing, drawing, etc.

flexibility: .... capacity to move a particular joint in the body through its range of motion

gross motor coordination: ..... development of the skeletal muscles to produce efficient total body movement

gross motor skills: .... movement involving the use of large and numerous muscles and not requiring as much precision as fine motor skills; includes actions such as walking, jumping, and throwing

haptic sense: .... integration of cutaneous (tactile) and kinesthetic information

hemiparesis: .... muscular weakness of one side of the body

hemiplegia: .... paralysis of one side of the body

hyperesthesia: .... increased sensitivity to touch hypertonia: .... greater than normal muscle tension

hypotonic: .... less than normal muscle tension

ipsilateral: .... occurring on one side of the body

kinesthesia: .... conscious perception of movement, weight, resistance, and position of a body part

locomotor movements: .... basic movements performed while moving the body on the feet from place to place

manipulative skills: .... combinations of fine and gross motor skills, usually involving the hands

modeling: .... setting an example for imitation

monoplegia: .... paralysis of one limb

motor planning: .... select group of movement skills combined to produce purposeful motor behavior

motor behavior: .... area of study of the psychological and physiological processes and mechanisms underlying motor performance

motor control: .... study of the neurophysiological factors that affect human movement

motor development: .... study of the changes in motor behavior occurring as a result of growth, maturation, and experience

motor learning: .... the continual process of extending children's initial concepts of movement

motor skills: .... specific set of movement responses requiring precision and accuracy for its accomplishment

motor task: .... specific movement skill or pattern designed and directed by the therapist for performance by the student

movement education: .... physical education approach utilizing basic movement patterns

movement exploration: .... method of teaching physical education through nondirective methods in which the participant explores the environment using basic movement patterns

movement flow: .... movement that is sequenced and conducted without hesitation

muscular endurance: .... capacity of the muscles to continue activity requiring muscular strength without undue fatigue

neuron: .... unit of the nervous system

ocular regressions: .... right-to-left movements of the eye made in a reverse direction during the reading process

open motor skill: .... skill that is performed in an unstable environment (the object or context changes during the performance of the skill), for example, in driving a car

paralysis: .... loss or impairment of motor and/or sensory function in a part of the body caused by injury to nerves or neurons

paraparesis: .... partial paralysis or weakness in lower extremities

paraplegia: .... paralysis of muscles in lower extremities

perception: .... mental process by which intellectual, sensory, and emotional data are organized meaningfully

performance: .... occurs after the learner translation and involves carrying out the specific skill

praxis: .... performance of a purposeful movement or group of movements; ability to motor plan and execute motor tasks

proprioception: .... appreciation of position, balance, and changes in equilibrium of a body part during movement by receiving stimulus within body tissue such as muscles, tendons, and joints

proximodistal rule: .... development of movement ability from the points close to the center of the body to the extreme points

purposeful activity: .... treatment that when directed to a response enhances neural integration

quadriparesis: .... partial paralysis or weakness in all four extremities

quadriplegia: .... paralysis of muscle in all four extremities

reflex: .... fetal or neonatal responses that are simple and predictable, resulting from tactile and vestibular stimulation

righting reactions: .... reflexes which through various receptors in the inner ear, eyes, muscles, or skin tend to bring an organism's body into its normal position in space and which resists any force acting to put it into a false position, for example, on its back

rigidity: .... inflexible and tonic contraction of muscles which gives consistent resistance to movement, from passive movement through total range of movement

self-image: .... psychological concept of an individual's perception of self as a person; it is one's own appraisal of one's personal worth and value and involves one's body image

sensory motor: .... integrating the senses and movement responses

serial motor skills: .... the combination of a few discrete motor skills in a sequence or series; for example, playing the piano requires striking specific keys for a certain period of time in a particular order

spastic: .... characterized by spasms and resulting in hypertonia and awkward movements from stiff muscles

spasticity: .... involuntary, velocity-dependent state of hypertonicity (increased muscle tone), resulting in resistance to movement; associated with exaggeration of reflexes and loss of voluntary muscle control

spatial relations: .... the relationship of the skeletal parts of the body to each other and to objects in the environment

static balance: .... balance in which the support is stable and the individual is not in locomotion

stereognosis: .... ability to recognize solid objects by using touch

tactile defensiveness: .... the quality of being unable to tolerate touch; being resistive and uncomfortable with certain kinds of touch (believed to be a form of sensory integrative dysfunction)

underreactive: .... responding minimally or slowly to stimuli

Terms Linking Motor and Academics

abdominal strength: .... the child's ability to demonstrate muscular contractions and endurance of the abdominal muscles

arm strength: .... the child's ability to demonstrate muscular contractions and endurance of the arms

audio-motor response: .... the child's ability to process auditory information and respond motorically

balance-postural orientation: the child's ability to balance in static and dynamic positions

color discrimination: .... the child's ability to distinguish different colors

endurance: .... the child's ability to maintain vigorous activity over relatively long periods of time

explosive leg power: .... the child's ability to demonstrate muscular contractions and endurance of the lower extremities

eye-foot accuracy: .... the child's ability to coordinate the eye and foot in motor tasks

eye-hand accuracy: .... the child's ability to use the eyes and hands efficiently in precise movements requiring the eyes and hands to work together

eye-hand coordination: .... the child's ability to use the eyes and hands efficiently in motor tasks

form discrimination: .... the child's ability to make a distinction between varieties of objects

gross body coordination: .... the child's ability to move the body, including arms, legs, and torso, efficiently when performing a motor task

kinesthetic-motor response: .. the child's ability to process information through the joints and maintain an appropriate position in space

language arts: .... the child's ability to participate in academic concepts while performing a motor task mathematics:.................................. the child's ability to carry out mathematical problems while performing a motor task

serialization:............................... the child's ability to perform a series of motor tasks in a sequence consistent with the directions provided

tactile-motor response: .... the child's ability to process tactile information and respond motorically

visual-motor response: .... the child's ability to process visual information and respond motorically

Glossary of Sensory Integration Terms

adaptive response: .... a suitable achievement in which the child responds effectively to environmental demands

body image: .... a child's feelings concerning his body

brain stem: .... the lowest and innermost portion of the brain; it is the center of thought and the organ that can perceive sensory information

cocontraction: .... the synchronized contraction of all muscles around a joint.

dyspraxia:................................ poor coordination displayed by some children, sometimes evident in poor handwriting and eye-hand coordination.

extension:................................ the movement of body parts that straighten out at the joints (the neck, arms, legs, etc.)

flexion: .... the movement of body parts that bend at the joints (neck, arms, legs, etc.)

gravitational insecurity:........... a child's apprehension related to head position; usually related to unclear messages from the vestibular and proprioceptive systems

hypersensitivity to movement: disorientation from vigorous activity in the form of headaches, nausea, and dizziness

kinesthesia: .... perception of the body in space from information received through the joints and muscles

lateralization: .... the localization of the control center in the brain for a particular function to be processed more on one side of the brain than the other

learning disorder:.................... a difficulty in learning to read, write, compute, or do schoolwork that cannot be attributed to impaired sight, hearing, or mental retardation

modulation:.............................. the brain's regulation of its own activity, involving facilitation of some neural messages to maximize a response, the inhibitism of other messages to reduce irrelevant activity

motor planning:....................... the child's ability to engage in activities in a sequential manner

prone: .... the child lying face down

nystagmus: .... a series of automatic, back-and-forth eye movements indicating impaired muscle function of the eye

occupational therapy: .... Occupational therapy is a health profession concerned with improving a person's occupational performance. In a pediatric setting, the occupational therapist deals with children whose occupations are usually players, preschoolers, or students. The occupational therapist evaluates a child's performance in relation to what is developmentally expected for that age group. If there is a discrepancy between developmental expectations and functional ability, the occupational therapist looks at a variety of perceptual and neuromuscular factors that influence function. Based on knowledge of neurology, kinesiology, development, medical diagnoses, and current research, the occupational therapist can identify the children who have the best potential for remediation through occupational therapy.

perception: .... the child's ability to process sensory information about the environment or from incoming stimuli

physical therapy: .... Physical therapy is a health profession concerned with improving a person's physical ability. In a pediatric setting, the physical therapist evaluates a child's orthopedic structure and neuromuscular functions. A physical therapist can also receive special training identical to that received by an occupational therapist to assess and remediate the disorders in sensory processing that influence learning and behavior.

praxis: .... performance of a purposeful movement or group of movements; ability to motor plan and execute motor tasks

proprioception: .... perception of sensory nerve endings in muscles, tendons, and joints that provides a sense of the body's position in space by responding to incoming stimuli.

sensory input: .... incoming stimuli from the senses to the brain and spinal cord

sensory integration: .... Sensory integration is the organization of sensory input for use. The "use" may be a perception of the body or the world, an adaptive response, a learning process, or the development of some neural function. Through sensory integration, the many parts of the nervous system work together so that a person can interact with the environment effectively and experience appropriate satisfaction.

sensory integrative dysfunction: ..an irregularity or disorder in brain function that makes it difficult to integrate sensory input effectively, may be present in motor, learning, social/emotional, speech/language, or attention disorders.

somatosensory: .... body sensations that are based on both tactile and proprioceptive information

specialization: .... in general, the manner in which one side of the brain more readily adapts than the other side to particular functions or conditions in response to environmental factors.

supine: .... the child lying on the back facing upward.

tactile:...................................... relating to the sense of touch

tactile defensiveness:............. a sensory integrative dysfunction in which tactile sensations create negative emotional reactions; it is associated with distractibility, restlessness, and behavior problems

vestibular system: .... the sensory system that responds to the position of the head in relation to gravity and accelerated or decelerated movement; integrates neck, eye, and body adjustments to movement

Developmental Milestones

1 Month:
- [ ] On back, head usually to one side
- [ ] On tummy, turns head when put down
- [ ] Looks at mobiles and faces
- [ ] Cuddles during feeding

2 Months:
- [ ] On back, turns head side to side
- [ ] On tummy, lifts head momentarily
- [ ] Eyes follow moving persons and objects
- [ ] Smiles responsively; coos

3 Months:
- [ ] On back, head more centered
- [ ] On tummy, lifts head two to three inches off crib surface
- [ ] Hands open most of the time
- [ ] Looks at hands
- [ ] Eyes focus on stationary objects
- [ ] Chuckles

4 Months:
- [ ] On back, head centered and hands together on chest
- [ ] On tummy, lifts head up and looks forward
- [ ] Plays with own fingers; grasps rattle
- [ ] Pulls clothes off face
- [ ] Babbles; smiles and vocalizes at mirror
- [ ] Rolls to side from back

5 Months:
- [ ] On back, lifts legs and sees feet
- [ ] Brings hands together for toys
- [ ] Rolls from back to tummy; on tummy, gets up on hands
- [ ] Takes weight on feet when standing
- [ ] Looks after dropped toy
- [ ] Laughs and squeals
- [ ] Discriminates between strangers and known persons
- [ ] Uses Palmer grasp—grasps objects against palm not using thumb
- [ ] Rolls side to side from a supine position

6 Months:
- [ ] Holds foot lying on back
- [ ] Rolls from tummy to back
- [ ] Sits with propping
- [ ] Shakes rattle; reaches for toy
- [ ] Pats self in mirror
- [ ] Tries out new sounds
- [ ] Holds head erect when sitting with support

7 Months:
- [ ] Puts feet in mouth
- [ ] Crawls on tummy; pivots in a circle on tummy
- [ ] Sits for a short time
- [ ] Mouths toys
- [ ] Bangs toys
- [ ] Transfers toys from hand to hand
- [ ] Imitates sounds
- [ ] Sits independently but may use hands

8 Months:
- [ ] Sits for a long time
- [ ] Stands holding on
- [ ] Holds two toys; drops toy on purpose
- [ ] Plays peekaboo
- [ ] Feeds self cracker; takes milk from cup
- [ ] Responds to name
- [ ] Rolls from supine to prone position

9 Months:
- [ ] Creeps on hands and knees
- [ ] Goes from sitting to tummy and tummy to sitting
- [ ] Bounces up and down while in a standing position
- [ ] Pokes at things with index finger
- [ ] Picks up small ball
- [ ] Plays patty-cake; waves bye-bye
- [ ] Uses radial digital grasp—grasp uses thumb, index, and middle finger—not palm
- [ ] Stands holding on

10 Months:
- [ ] Pulls up to stand in crib
- [ ] Gets down from standing
- [ ] Says "da da" and "ma ma"
- [ ] Understands "no"
- [ ] Hugs and loves toy
- [ ] Offers toy to others
- [ ] Pushes arms through armsholes when dressing
- [ ] Uses inferior pincer grasp—index, thumb, using lower part of index finger
- [ ] Crawls on all fours (reciprocally)

11 Months:
- [ ] Walks around furniture
- [ ] Walks with two hands held
- [ ] Pivots when sitting
- [ ] Picks up small block; gives toy when asked
- [ ] Lifts blanket to find toy
- [ ] Says two to three "words"
- [ ] Lifts feet for dressing
- [ ] Drinks from cup
- [ ] Reaches sitting position by self

12 Months:
- [ ] Stands alone momentarily
- [ ] Squats to play
- [ ] Makes steps from one object to another
- [ ] Picks up small cracker
- [ ] Grasps crayon in fist and imitates scribbling
- [ ] Says four to six "words"
- [ ] Pats pictures in books; communicates by pointing
- [ ] Plays ball with others
- [ ] Assumes and maintains kneeling
- [ ] Walks with one hand held
- [ ] Uses neat pincer grasp—grasps with precise thumb and finger opposition
- [ ] Crawls with coordination
- [ ] Creeps on plantigrade feet and hands
- [ ] Exhibits hopping and staggering reactions
- [ ] Rolls ball forward from sitting position

15 Months:
- [ ] Walks alone and seldom falls; runs stiffly
- [ ] Squats to play; stands up from squat
- [ ] Walks upstairs with one hand held
- [ ] Climbs on chair to reach things
- [ ] Hurls ball
- [ ] Scribbles spontaneously
- [ ] Has a 10 to 20 word vocabulary
- [ ] Feeds with spoon, but spills
- [ ] Plays with pull toys
- [ ] Points to two of own body parts

18 Months:
- [ ] Walks downstairs with one hand held
- [ ] "Walks" into large ball to kick; tries to jump
- [ ] Turns two to three pages together
- [ ] Likes to stack a few blocks
- [ ] Points to own nose, eyes, hair, and mouth
- [ ] Has a 20 to 30 word vocabulary
- [ ] Asks for "more" and "drink"

- [ ] Drinks well from a cup and uses a spoon; puts on hat; takes off socks
- [ ] Imitates mom and dad in play; seats self in small chair
- [ ] Hurls ball from standing position without falling
- [ ] Log rolls
- [ ] Stands on one foot with help

2 Years:
- [ ] Runs well; walks up- and downstairs holding on
- [ ] Jumps down from bottom step
- [ ] Kicks large ball; throws ball forward
- [ ] Imitates vertical stroke and circular scribble
- [ ] Turns book pages one at a time
- [ ] Unscrews some parts of toys
- [ ] Vocabulary has too many words to count
- [ ] Points to body parts; names at least one
- [ ] Likes pretend play; feeds doll
- [ ] Likes to help around house
- [ ] Identifies self in mirror
- [ ] Uses palmer supinate grasp
- [ ] Stoops and recovers
- [ ] Walks backward
- [ ] Walks upstairs and downstairs alone without alternating feet
- [ ] Identifies two body parts from picture

2 1/2 Years:
- [ ] Jumps with both feet off floor
- [ ] Tries to stand on one foot
- [ ] Alternates feet going upstairs
- [ ] Imitates horizontal stroke; imitates circle
- [ ] Pours liquid from glass to glass
- [ ] Names seven body parts
- [ ] Expresses self in three to four word sentences
- [ ] Answers simple questions—"What does a doggie say?"
- [ ] Knows "big" and "little"
- [ ] Pulls up pants; finds armholes correctly
- [ ] Puts shoes on, not necessarily on correct feet
- [ ] Stands on one foot with help

3 Years:
- [ ] Rides tricycle using pedals
- [ ] Goes downstairs alternating feet
- [ ] Stands on one foot for two to three seconds
- [ ] Walks on tiptoes
- [ ] Throws overhand
- [ ] Holds crayons with fingers
- [ ] Copies circle; draws vertical and horizontal lines
- [ ] Tries to cut with scissors

- ☐ Knows "up" and "down," "loud" and "soft"
- ☐ Matches colors and identifies two colors
- ☐ Likes to play with other children
- ☐ Understands taking turns; likes to "make believe"
- ☐ Washes and dries hands
- ☐ Digital pronate grasp
- ☐ Jumps on both feet
- ☐ Jumps from 12-inch height, one foot leading
- ☐ Walks upstairs alternating feet

3 1/2 Years:
- ☐ Builds tower with 9 to 10 one-inch cubes
- ☐ Catches bounced ball
- ☐ Folds a sheet of paper
- ☐ Draws any two parts of a six-part stick figure
- ☐ Identifies 6 to 10 body parts
- ☐ Stands on tiptoes for ten seconds
- ☐ Stands on one foot alone for one to two seconds

4 Years:
- ☐ Marches rhythmically to music
- ☐ Hops on one foot; tries to skip
- ☐ Positions arms to catch ball
- ☐ Copies a cross (+)
- ☐ Tries to cut on a line; likes to paint
- ☐ Uses words like "pretty," "big," and "happy" appropriately
- ☐ Counts to five; uses eight to nine word sentences
- ☐ Repeats all of a nursery rhyme or song
- ☐ Dresses self except for tying bows
- ☐ Puts shoes on correct feet
- ☐ Likes to make things from clay or blocks
- ☐ Plays with children in a group
- ☐ Runs smoothly at different speeds
- ☐ Bounces ball to self and catches it
- ☐ Catches object tossed by another person
- ☐ Uses static tripod posture
- ☐ Stands on one foot for three to eight seconds
- ☐ Walks downstairs alternating feet
- ☐ Broad jumps 8 to 10-inches from 2 feet
- ☐ Hops on one foot
- ☐ Runs smoothly at different speeds
- ☐ Draws any four parts of a six-part stick figure (4 ½ years)

5 Years:
- ☐ "Gallops" to skip; plays on monkey bars
- ☐ Tries to turn somersaults
- ☐ Rides bicycle with training wheels
- ☐ Catches large ball with two hands
- ☐ Copies a square and a triangle

- ☐ Likes cutting, pasting, and coloring
- ☐ Draws picture of a man with body; counts to ten
- ☐ Names five colors; prints name
- ☐ Knows what one plus one equals, and what one plus two equals
- ☐ Likes puzzles and matching shapes
- ☐ Ties shoes
- ☐ Likes school
- ☐ Throws ball up to self and catches it
- ☐ Throws with some control
- ☐ Uses dynamic tripod posture
- ☐ Stands on one foot alone eight to ten seconds
- ☐ Jumps 10-inch high hurdle from standing position
- ☐ Copies Simon Says postures
- ☐ Knows front, back, and side of self – chin, neck, and forearm
- ☐ Draws six-part recognizable person with a body
- ☐ Holds prone extension (Superman) for 10 seconds
- ☐ Walks on 12-inch line for 12 feet – heel to toe
- ☐ Dribbles an 8-inch ball with one hand
- ☐ Strikes ball on string with bat
- ☐ Crumples a piece of paper into a ball
- ☐ Points front, back, near, up, and down with eyes closed
- ☐ Knows some body part functions
- ☐ Knows all body parts

6 Years:
- ☐ Skips
- ☐ Broad jumps 3 feet from standing
- ☐ Dribbles ball with one hand with control
- ☐ Copies Simon Says postures crossing the midline
- ☐ Throws at advanced level
- ☐ Jumps over 15-inch-high rope

7 Years:
- ☐ Holds crouched position on tip-toes
- ☐ Arises from supine position to standing in 1 to 1.5 seconds
- ☐ Jumps ropes without assistance
- ☐ Catches a tennis ball with one hand
- ☐ Knows left/right concepts on self

Getting Started

Positive movement experiences can make a real contribution to the cognitive, social, and emotional development of young children. Children succeed when they are engaged in developmentally-appropriate gross motor activities. In addition, allowing children to explore movement freely encourages them to learn new ways to move; these movements can then be integrated into planned motor acts. The following are some simple practices to guide these early movement activities:

1. **There is no right or wrong way in which a child responds to movement cues.**
   Begin by experiencing the movement before you ask children to perform it. Then, have children move their bodies and explore "how" they move through their senses. Do not be concerned with the quality of their movements; movement itself is the goal.

2. **Each movement experience is exploratory.**
   Children develop at different rates. Allow children to explore the movement activity to the best of their abilities and with their own individual levels of success.

3. **Movement experiences can enhance a child's positive self-image.**
   Because movement is personal and success depends upon each child's abilities, be sure to provide plenty of positive reinforcement as children explore and expand their movement skills.

4. **Each child needs to learn and move at his own pace (not ours).**
   It is important as educators to recognize that it is not our responsibility to remake a child into someone he is not. Teachers should engage students in physical activity, allowing them to develop individually with success and fun!

5. **Continuity, repetition, and experience are the concrete base for the learning of motor skills.**
   Movement experiences should not be left to just recess and physical education programs. Instead, movement should be part of the overall curriculum and provided in numerous daily opportunities within the framework of the classroom.

6. **Using music allows and assists the child to recognize that the activity has a beginning and an end.**
   Rhythms and music have a profound impact on children. Using music to promote physical activity benefits the child enormously by developing the very important concept of closure. The closure can begin to lay the foundation for developing organizational skills.

7. **Administer stimulation using one modality—aural decoding, visual decoding, or tactile/kinesthetic decoding—at a time.**
   Children are continually processing sensory information. When presenting a new activity, it is best to use one modality to introduce the movement. For example, if you would like to have children learn a new marching step, it is best to describe the step to them without demonstrating the movement (auditory processing). Then, when actually demonstrating the movement, do not speak. Let children visually process the information without having to decode the auditory information at the same time. For children who have difficulty processing the information separately, a tactile approach may be needed to assist them in the acquisition of the skill (kinesthetic/proprioception).

8. **Employ recall.**
   After movement experiences, ask children to tell what they did with their bodies. This is an outstanding opportunity for children to build their vocabularies by first engaging in movement and then describing both the movement and how they felt when they were moving. This will allow for language stimulation as well as to connect the motor skill with language acquisition. This practice also provides a foundation for the development of comprehension skills—invaluable skills as children become readers.

Global Movement Experiences

Movement experiences can enhance each child's school performance. These experiences in movement can help children to succeed in school because they can:

- provide movement exploration coordination for the child who is learning physically,
- develop the child's body awareness, body scheme, and space awareness,
- enhance the child's attending skills by providing movement experiences that strengthen aural comprehension and visual perception skills, and, perhaps most importantly,
- help the child develop a positive self-esteem.

Building "Rock Solid" Foundations for Learning

In light of classroom demands driven by high-powered curriculums, it is critical to understand the human body and how it develops. If the gross motor development of a child is compromised, the fine motor domain can be negatively affected as well. As we continue to increase expectations in the classroom, we may be missing the most important link to success: building a "rock solid" foundation for learning by developing gross motor skills.

Here is a closer look at how the human body develops:

From Simple to More Complex

static movement .... dynamic movement

movement touching the body .... movement away from the body

movement of the trunk........... movement of the limbs .... movement of the fingers and toes

gross motor movement .... fine motor movement

nonlocomotor movement .... locomotor movement... .... integrated movement

movement without an object .... movement with an object

symmetrical movement .... asymmetrical movement

bilateral movement .... movement on either one side or the other........ alternating movement

single movement........................... sequenced movement............ .... tracking movement

personal space.. general space

When creating gross motor activities for children, the above psychomotor skills should take place in an organized and sequential manner. Engaging children in gross motor activities will stimulate growth in all of these areas and will begin to prepare the foundation they need to successfully master the classroom's fine motor demands.

Successful Strategies in the Classroom

The following are some general teaching techniques:

1. Plan the sequence of activities to progress from simple to more complex and within students' ability levels.

2. When working with a new group of students, begin slowly and gradually introduce them to more complex activities. Keep in mind students may fear new movement activities and may become embarrassed or display a lack of initiative.

3. Movement is observable. Help all students to be sensitive to others and explain that each student is unique and moves at his own pace. Utilize activities—developmentally appropriate tasks—that result in personal feelings of achievement.

4. Offer continuous and immediate positive reinforcement when students are engaged in movement, regardless of the "quality" of their movements.

5. Provide a calm, inviting, nonthreatening environment in which to learn.

6. Use clear, simple, and concise directions and remember to separate modalities.

7. Decrease the distractions in the instructional environment.

8. Maintain eye contact and/or proximal distance to students when giving directions.

9. Many students are accustomed to learning through modeling. It is desirable, however, for them to respond to verbal cues. Use demonstrations and manipulations when necessary. But, as you teach, mentally record whether students understand the directions so that you can provide the best opportunity for them to learn through visual, auditory, or tactile stimulation or any combination of these methods.

10. Use a variety of teaching techniques to find what works best with each individual student's learning style.

11. Provide information appropriate to students' cognitive abilities.

12. Determine the amount of assistance each student needs. If a greater level of assistance is needed, the game or activity may not be developmentally appropriate.

13. Instruct students in safety procedures. Always check the instructional environment for safety hazards.

14. Begin activities at lower skill levels and progressively increase skill requirements for students to become successful.

15. When appropriate, involve students in the decision-making process of game and activity modifications.

16. If you have a student with special needs, consult with your school's occupational or physical therapist for modifications and adaptations so that every student can achieve success.

17. Consult with the physical education or adapted physical education teacher for more ideas.

Game and Activity Modifications

There are a variety of ways to modify a game or an activity to include all of the students within a class. To achieve full participation of all students, the teacher must be sensitive to their range of abilities. Modifying and adapting games and activities accommodates varying skill levels and can enhance each student's ability to participate and achieve success in movement. If a planned movement activity uses equipment, frequently the equipment can be modified to accommodate the developmental needs of students, especially the very young.

Here are some suggested modifications:

1. Change the size of balls, hoops, ropes, etc.
2. Change the weight of the balls.
3. Change the color and texture of balls, beanbags, etc.
4. Change bats, rackets, and other equipment to a lighter weight and/or size.
5. Change the size of the area of play.
6. Change the time requirement for the specified skill (for example, hopping on one foot).
7. Mark off the children's play area with cones or markers.

Here are some more general modifications to ensure each student's success:

1. Change the method of locomotion to be used (for example, running, walking, or crawling).
2. Change the number of persons participating (for example, individual, partners, small group, or teams).
3. Consider the number of repetitions, distance traveled, or trials allowed.
4. Change from standing to sitting or lying down.
5. Change from kicking to striking.
6. Reduce the period of time the game or activity is played.
7. Adapt games to make them nonelimination.
8. Reduce the amount of action required.
9. Set time limits based on students' abilities, interest, or endurance.
10. Vary the tempo of the activity often.
11. Determine the "fitness" level of students and provide a rest period within the game's playing time.
12. If you have a physically challenged student, consult the school's occupational or physical therapist for modifications and adaptation ideas.
13. If necessary, demonstrate the movement skill needed to play.
14. Use students with higher skills as peer buddies to assist others in the game or activity.
15. Rotate players so that everyone has a chance to be the leader in the game or activity.

The Importance of Gross Motor Movement in the Development of Cognitive Skills

The games and activities presented in *Gross Motor Fun* include a wide range of movement opportunities that allow students to develop important perceptual motor skills. Many of these skills can be addressed daily, simply by allowing children to play outdoors in a variety of activities. Increasing muscular endurance and strength in gross motor activities also enable students to progress to greater motor control for fine motor activities.

Providing these motor components enhances the learning process. The following matrix highlights and defines key perceptual motor skills and describes how the lack of these motor skills can impact a child's ability to learn.

Perceptual Motor Skills	Definition	Classroom Impact
Figure-Ground Discrimination	The ability to see specific figures even when they are hidden in confusing and complex backgrounds	❏ Gives poor attention to detail ❏ Often appears disoriented ❏ Is careless when reading; may skip words or lines ❏ Struggles to solve problems if too much is written on a page
Form Consistency	The ability to match two figures that vary on one or more than one discriminating features (size, position, shade, etc.)	❏ Confuses letters, e.g., *I = n, v = u, c = e* ❏ Confuses differences in written forms, e.g., own writing and text of a book ❏ Confuses words of similar appearance, e.g., *how = now, canary = carry*
Spatial Relationships	The ability to match two figures according to their common features (object and self)	❏ Has difficulty with spelling, e.g., *house = huose, field = feild* ❏ Writes words in incorrect sequence, e.g., *He went to town. = He to town went.* ❏ Has difficulty in math; writes numbers incorrectly, e.g., 14 = 41 ❏ Is unable to follow events in a logical sequence resulting in difficulty following instructions
Position in Space	The ability to connect dots to reproduce visually presented patterns (between two objects)	❏ Creates work that is topsy-turvy ❏ Is often clumsy and hesitant to perform tasks ❏ Reverses letters and numbers, e.g., *b = d, p = q, 62 = 26* ❏ Concepts of left and right are not easily understood, resulting in difficulties in math

Visual Motor Coordination	The ability of the hands to carry out the movement idea in the brain in a dexterous manner	❑ Has difficulty with dressing and self-care activities ❑ Has difficulty with kicking, throwing, and catching ❑ Has difficulty with writing, drawing, and cutting ❑ Has difficulty with copying
Lateralization	The ability to differentiate between left and right and apply that knowledge; the ability to use both sides of the body automatically	❑ Lacks understanding of spatial concepts ❑ Confuses left and right; has difficulty following instructions, e.g., "Begin in the top left corner." ❑ Has difficulty reading since the ability to work from left to right and top to bottom is essential
Crossing the Midline	The ability to use each side of the body independently as a whole in a dexterous manner; the integration of the use of both sides of the body	❑ Exhibits clumsiness with jerky movements and lack of coordination ❑ Works only to the right of the midline if right-handed and to the left of the midline if left-handed ❑ Shifts the body to keep the hand to the right or left of the body, depending upon handedness ❑ In severe cases, transfers a pencil or crayon to the other hand when reaching the midline ❑ Shifts the paper when writing or drawing
Visual Memory	The ability to recall visual stimuli in terms of form, position, sequence, etc., on both a short- and long-term basis	❑ Makes poor academic progress ❑ Incorrectly copies off of the board ❑ Has spelling difficulties
Visual Memory Integration	The degree to which visual perception and motor behavior are integrated	❑ Is unable to associate a particular series of movements with specific visual patterns ❑ Knows what must be done but cannot ideate the motor plan ❑ Has difficulty copying words, numbers, or forms
Attention and Concentration	The ability to focus on the task at hand for a suitable period of time	❑ Is easily distracted by external noise or activity ❑ Is a "dreamer," distracted by own thoughts
Hypotonic	Low muscle tone; uses up energy and concentration on adjusting posture and not on learning	❑ Slouches ❑ Tires easily ❑ Continually shifts positions

Let's Get Moving!

Movement experiences can enhance cognitive learning. In addition, your classroom is made up of children who learn in a variety of different ways, including visual, linguistic, auditory, and physical learners. *Gross Motor Fun* will allow you to focus on the physical learners, an area of intelligence that is often overlooked.

Physical learners can be separated into two areas: the tactile (touch) and the kinesthetic (movement). Often undiagnosed and labeled as hyperactive, these students receive information from the environment through receptors in the skin and the joints, muscles, and tendons. Physical learners need to explore their world through touch and/or movement and may have difficulty sitting for long periods in the classroom.

Utilizing the activities in this book meets the needs of these students as they attempt to achieve academic and curriculum goals. When students have difficulty processing visual and/or auditory information during instruction (for example, the difference between a square and rectangle), they may be well served by handling the actual objects or walking the outlines of the shapes on the floor. Providing gross motor activities daily gives physical learners another opportunity to succeed in the classroom by using their strengths.

Incorporating multiple ways to approach the curriculum also helps to meet the requirements of children with special needs who are included within the general education classroom. Because these students may also have a variety of different learning styles, the activities in *Gross Motor Fun* will provide another opportunity to meet the needs of all students.

The variety of games and activities presented in the following chapters can form a base of movement experiences for your students. Select those activities that are developmentally appropriate for students' cognitive, emotional, and physical abilities. In addition, as you explore these games, use your imagination and creativity to design other games that include the developmental academic concepts on which your students are working.

Chapter 1: Tag, You're It!

Tag games have been around for years, and children continue to enjoy them tremendously. Improved fundamental gross motor movements, increased fitness and other health-related benefits, and the strengthening of spatial-body perceptual skills are just some of the positive effects of playing tag. This chapter contains a wide variety of tag games that contribute to the development of gross motor skills while enhancing the learning process.

Early Learning and Movement Tag Games

Animal Walk Tag

Equipment: none

Task Analysis: arm strength, abdominal strength, muscular strength and endurance, cardiorespiratory endurance, lateralization, crossing the midline, visual memory, figure-ground discrimination, hypotonic

Description: This tag game requires students to perform different animal walks after they have been tagged. First, select an animal (e.g., a bear) and choose a student to be the tagger. Children begin to walk through the play space as the tagger performs the selected animal walk (e.g., bear walk) and attempts to tag the other children. When a child is tagged, that child must also perform the animal walk as she moves through the play space assisting the original tagger. The game continues until all children are performing the animal walk.

Have students try to move like these animals: crab, kangaroo, bunny, seal, inchworm, bear, frog, duck, elephant, horse, and caterpillar. You may also use movements of the types of animals you are currently studying in the classroom.

Variations: When the tagger tags a student, the tagged student calls out a new animal. All other players then begin to move like the new animal. A student can be safe from being tagged if that student makes the continuous sound of the selected animal (e.g., growls like a bear).

Animal Walk Tag—Form Discrimination

Equipment: stuffed animals and/or pictures of animals (animal action cards can be found on pages 142–145)

Task Analysis: arm strength, abdominal strength, muscular strength and endurance, cardiorespiratory endurance, form discrimination, picture identification, visual memory, figure-ground discrimination, form constancy, spatial relationships, position in space, attention and concentration, hypotonic

Description: Begin by placing the stuffed animals or displaying the animal pictures throughout the play space. Then, hold up a selected animal (e.g., an elephant) and choose a student to be the tagger. Children begin to walk through the play space as the tagger performs the selected animal walk (e.g., elephant walk). Students may walk to and touch the stuffed selected animal or picture of the animal to avoid being tagged. When a child is tagged, that child must also perform the animal walk as he moves through the play space assisting the original tagger. The game continues until all children are performing the animal walk. Have students try to move like these animals: crab, kangaroo, bunny, seal, inchworm, bear, frog, duck, elephant, horse, and caterpillar. You may also use movements of the types of animals you are currently studying in the classroom.

Locomotor Tag

Equipment: none

Task Analysis: arm strength, abdominal strength, muscular strength and endurance, cardiorespiratory endurance, bilateral activities, locomotor skills, lateralization, crossing the midline, hypotonic

Description: This tag game allows students to explore the movement of different locomotor skills. First, select the locomotor skill to be performed (e.g., galloping) as well as the number of times to circle the play area. Choose a student to be the tagger. All of the children move through the play space performing the selected locomotor skill. The tagger begins to try to tag other students. When a child is tagged, that child must circle the play area while performing a different locomotor skill the specified number of times. After completing the movement, the child reenters the game. Remember to choose a new tagger often.

Body Part Partner Tag

Equipment: none

Task Analysis: arm strength, abdominal strength, muscular strength and endurance, cardiorespiratory endurance, bilateral activities, identification of body parts, crossing the midline, lateralization, locomotor skills, socialization, hypotonic

Description: This traditional tag game allows students to identify body parts. First, select the body part (e.g., elbow) to touch with a partner. Designate a locomotor skill to be performed (e.g., leaping) or an animal walk (e.g., crab walk), as well as the required number of times to circle the play area. Choose a student to be the tagger. All of the children move through the play space performing the selected locomotor skill or animal walk. The tagger begins to try to tag other students. To avoid being tagged, students may find partners and touch the selected body parts. When a child is tagged, that child must circle the play area while performing a different locomotor skill the specified number of times. After completing the movement, the child reenters the game. Remember to choose a new tagger often.

Body Part Tag

Equipment: none

Task Analysis: arm strength, abdominal strength, muscular strength and endurance, cardiorespiratory endurance, bilateral activities, locomotor skills, cognition, visual memory, visual discrimination, body part awareness, body part function, figure-ground discrimination, form constancy, spatial relationships, position in space, attention and concentration, hypotonic

Description: This tag game allows students to identify body parts. First, select two body parts (e.g., right elbow and left knee). Designate a locomotor skill to be performed (e.g., taking giant steps) or an animal walk (e.g., crab walk) as well as the number of times to circle the play area. Choose a student to be the tagger. All of the children move through the play space performing the selected locomotor skill or animal walk. The tagger begins to try to tag other students. To avoid being tagged, a child may touch together the selected body parts (e.g., touch her right elbow to her left knee). When a child is tagged, that child must circle the play area while performing a different locomotor skill the specified number of times. After completing the movement, the child reenters the game. Remember to choose a new tagger often.

◆▼●■★◆▼●■★◆▼●■★◆▼●■★◆▼●■★◆▼●■★◆▼●■★◆▼●■★◆▼●■★◆▼●■★◆▼

Body Shape Letter Tag

Equipment: upper- and lowercase letter cards (found on pages 33–41)

Task Analysis: muscular strength and endurance, cardiorespiratory endurance, language arts, upper- and lowercase letter identification, form discrimination, visual memory, locomotor skills, body awareness, socialization, figure-ground discrimination, form constancy, spatial relationships, position in space, attention and concentration, crossing the midline, lateralization, hypotonic

Description: This tag game allows students to recognize and identify upper- and lowercase letters by forming the shapes of the letters with their bodies. Designate the locomotor skill to be performed (e.g., sideways slide) or an animal walk (e.g., inchworm inch) as well as the number of times to circle the play area. Choose a student to be the tagger. Then, hold up a selected letter card and say the letter aloud. The tagger begins to try to tag other students. To avoid being tagged, students may make the shape of the selected letter with their bodies. If a child is tagged before forming the selected letter, that child must circle the play area, performing a different locomotor skill the specified number of times. After completing the movement, the child reenters the game. Remember to choose a new tagger often

Number or Letter Partner Tag

Equipment: letter cards (found on pages 33–41), number cards (found on pages 53–56)

Task Analysis: arm strength, abdominal strength, muscular strength and endurance, cardiorespiratory endurance, bilateral activities, locomotor skills, cognition, visual memory, visual discrimination, body part awareness, figure-ground discrimination, form constancy, spatial relationships, position in space, attention and concentration, crossing the midline, lateralization, hypotonic

Description: This traditional tag game allows students to recognize and identify letters and numbers by forming the shapes of the letters and numbers with their bodies. Designate the locomotor skill to be performed (e.g., leaping) or an animal walk (e.g., panther slink) as well as the number of times to circle the play area. Choose a student to be the tagger and have each child select a partner and hold hands. Partners will stay connected as they move through the play space. Then, hold up a selected letter or number card and say the letter or number aloud. The tagger begins to try to tag other students. To avoid being tagged, the pairs of students may make the shape of the selected letter or number with their bodies. If a pair of students is tagged before forming the selected letter, they must circle the play area, performing a different locomotor skill the specified number of times. After completing the movement, the students reenter the game. Remember to choose a new tagger often.

Yoga Tag

Equipment: pictures of selected yoga poses (yoga poses cards found on pages 26–27)

Task Analysis: arm strength, abdominal strength, muscular strength and endurance, cardiorespiratory endurance, bilateral activities, static balance, laterality, body awareness, locomotor skills, visual memory, figure-ground discrimination, form constancy, spatial relationships, position in space, attention and concentration, hypotonic

Description: This traditional tag game allows students to develop body awareness, static balance, and muscular endurance and strength. First, select a yoga pose pictured on a card. Designate a locomotor skill to be performed (e.g., dancing) or an animal walk (e.g., kangaroo hop) as well as the number of times to circle the play area. Choose a student to be the tagger. All of the children move through the play space performing the selected locomotor skill or animal walk. The tagger begins to try to tag other students. To avoid being tagged, students may demonstrate the yoga pose. When a child is tagged, that child must circle the play area, performing a different locomotor skill the specified number of times. After completing the movement, the child reenters the game. Remember to choose a new tagger often.

Sit Position – Sukhasana

Dog and Cat

Mountain – Tadasana

The Triangle – Trikonasana

Warrior II - Virabhadrasana II

The Cobra - Bhujangasana

Half Shoulder Stand - Araha Sarvangasana

The Bridge - Sethu Bandhasana

Color Tag

Equipment: cards in a variety of colors

Task Analysis: muscular strength and endurance, cardiorespiratory endurance, language arts, color recognition, visual memory, locomotor skills, figure-ground discrimination, form constancy, spatial relationships, position in space, attention and concentration, hypotonic

Description: This tag game allows students to recognize and identify selected colors. Begin by scattering the color cards throughout the play space. Designate the locomotor skill to be performed (e.g., walking backwards) as well as the number of times to circle the play area. Choose a student to be the tagger. Then, hold up a selected color. The tagger begins to try to tag other students. To avoid being tagged, students may find and touch with their toes a card of the selected color. When a child is tagged, that child must circle the play area, performing the designated locomotor skill the specified number of times. After completing the movement, the child reenters the game. Remember to choose a new tagger often.

Variation: Use a variety of shape cards in various colors instead of color cards. This will challenge students to focus on one attribute (color) even when it is presented in a variety of familiar shapes.

Color Balloon Tag

Equipment: color word flash cards, inflated colorful balloons

Caution: Before completing any balloon activity, ask families about possible latex allergies. Also, remember that uninflated or popped balloons may present a choking hazard.

Task Analysis: arm strength, abdominal strength, muscular strength and endurance, cardiorespiratory endurance, bilateral activities, locomotor skills, cognition, visual memory, visual discrimination, body part function, color discrimination, eye-hand coordination, crossing the midline, attention and concentration, lateralization, hypotonic

Description: This tag game allows students to recognize and identify colors. Begin by scattering the colorful inflated balloons throughout the play space. Designate the locomotor skill to be performed (e.g., marching) or an animal walk (e.g., horse gallop) as well as the number of times to circle the play area. Choose a student to be the tagger. Then, hold up a color word flash card and read the word aloud. The tagger begins to try to tag other students. To avoid being tagged, students may find a balloon of the selected color and tap it repeatedly to keep it aloft. When a child is tagged, that child must circle the play area, performing a different locomotor skill the specified number of times. After completing the movement, the child reenters the game. Remember to choose a new tagger often.

Shape Tag

Equipment: shape cards in one color

Task Analysis: muscular strength and endurance, cardiorespiratory endurance, language arts, visual-discrimination, visual memory, locomotor skills, figure-ground discrimination, form constancy, spatial relationships, position in space, attention and concentration, hypotonic

Description: This traditional tag game allows students to recognize and identify selected shapes. Begin by scattering the shape cards throughout the play space. Designate the locomotor skill to be performed (e.g., marching) as well as the number of times to circle the play area. Choose a student to be the tagger. Then, hold up a selected shape. The tagger begins to try to tag other students. To avoid being tagged, students may find and touch with their toes a card of the selected shape. When a child is tagged, that child must circle the play area, performing the designated locomotor skill the specified number of times. After completing the movement, the child reenters the game. Remember to choose a new tagger often.

Variation: Use a variety of shape cards in various colors. This will challenge students to focus on one attribute (shape) even when it is presented in a variety of colors.

Same or Different Tag

Equipment: two sets of cards featuring numbers (found on pages 53–56), letter cards (found on pages 33–41), or picture cards (found on pages 29–31). Make two copies of each card.

Task Analysis: arm strength, abdominal strength, muscular strength and endurance, cardiorespiratory endurance, bilateral activities, language arts, antonyms, visual memory, locomotor skills, figure-ground discrimination, form constancy, spatial relationships, position in space, math, visual discrimination, hypotonic

Description: This traditional tag game allows students to develop the concept of same or different. Begin by scattering one set of cards featuring numbers, letters, or pictures throughout the play space. Designate the locomotor skill to be performed (e.g., skipping) or an animal walk (e.g., snake slither) as well as the number of times a student who is tagged must circle the play area. Choose a student to be the tagger. Then, hold up a selected card from the other matching set of cards. The tagger begins to try to tag other students. To avoid being tagged, students may find and touch with their toes the number, letter, or picture card that is the same as the selected card. When a child is tagged, that child must circle the play area, performing a different locomotor skill the specified number of times. After completing the movement, the child reenters the game. Remember to choose a new tagger often.

(picture cards)

Language Arts Tag Games

Letter Tag

Equipment: letter cards (found on pages 33–41)

Task Analysis: muscular strength and endurance, cardiorespiratory endurance, language arts, letter recognition, visual memory, locomotor skills, figure-ground discrimination, form constancy, spatial relationships, position in space, attention and concentration, hypotonic

Description: This tag game allows students to recognize and identify selected letters of the alphabet. Begin by scattering the letter cards throughout the play space. Designate the locomotor skill to be performed (e.g., skipping) as well as the number of times to circle the play area. Choose a student to be the tagger. Then, hold up a selected letter or letters. The tagger begins to try to tag other students. To avoid being tagged, students may find and touch with their toes a card with the selected letter(s). When a child is tagged, that child must circle the play area, performing the designated locomotor skill the specified number of times. After completing the movement, the child reenters the game. Remember to choose a new tagger often.

Letter Sound Tag

Equipment: letter cards (found on pages 33–41)

Task Analysis: muscular strength and endurance, cardiorespiratory endurance, language arts, letter sound recognition, visual memory, locomotor skills, figure-ground discrimination, form constancy, spatial relationships, position in space, attention and concentration, hypotonic

Description: This tag game allows students to recognize and identify the alphabet letters that make the selected sounds. Begin by scattering the letter cards throughout the play space. Designate the locomotor skill to be performed (e.g., galloping) as well as the number of times to circle the play area. Choose a student to be the tagger. Then, hold up a selected letter and review the sound of the letter. The tagger begins to try to tag other students. To avoid being tagged, students may find and touch with their toes a card with the letter that makes the selected sound. When a child is tagged, that child must circle the play area, performing the designated locomotor skill the specified number of times. After completing the movement, the child reenters the game. Remember to choose a new tagger often.

Upper- and Lowercase Letter Tag

Equipment: upper- and lowercase letter cards (found on pages 33–41)

Task Analysis: muscular strength and endurance, cardiorespiratory endurance, language arts, upper- and lowercase letter identification, form discrimination, visual memory, locomotor skills, figure-ground discrimination, form constancy, spatial relationships, position in space, attention and concentration, hypotonic

Description: This tag game allows students to recognize, identify, and match the uppercase and the lowercase forms of selected letters of the alphabet. Begin by scattering the letter cards throughout the play space. Designate the locomotor skill to be performed (e.g., tiptoeing) as well as the number of times to circle the play area. Choose a student to be the tagger. Then, hold up a selected letter and review whether it is the upper- or lowercase form of the letter. The tagger begins to try to tag other students. To avoid being tagged, students may find and touch with their toes a card with the selected letter in the form that was not previously shown, either upper- or lowercase. When a child is tagged, that child must circle the play area, performing the designated locomotor skill the specified number of times. After completing the movement, the child reenters the game. Remember to choose a new tagger often.

A a

B b

C c

D   d

E   e

F   f

G g

H h

I i

◆▼●■★◆▼●■★◆▼●■★◆▼●■★◆▼●■★◆▼●■★◆▼●■★◆▼●■★◆▼●■★◆▼●■★◆▼

J

j

K

k

L

l

M m

N n

O o

P

p

Q

q

R

r

S   s

T   t

U   U

V v

W w

X X

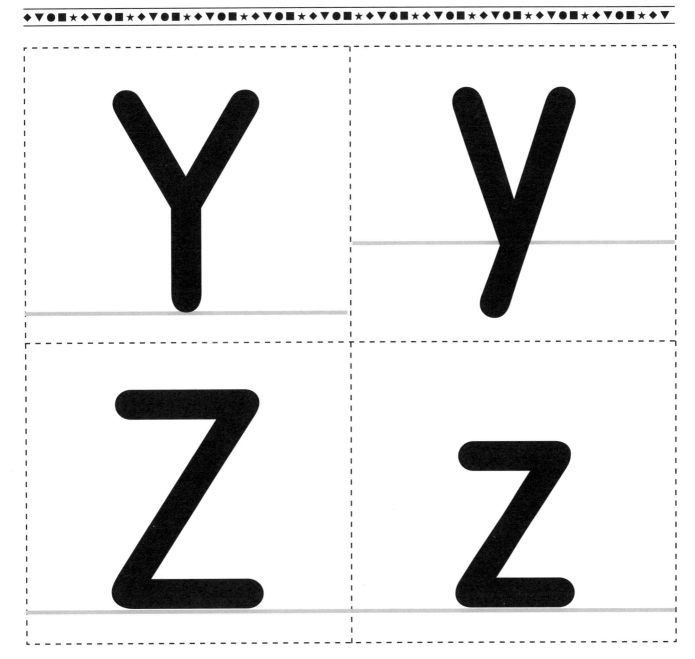

Find Your Name Tag

Equipment: cards labeled with students' names

Task Analysis: muscular strength and endurance, cardiorespiratory endurance, language arts, name recognition, visual memory, locomotor skills, figure-ground discrimination, form constancy, spatial relationships, position in space, attention and concentration, hypotonic

Description: This tag game allows students to recognize and identify their own names. Begin by scattering the name cards throughout the play space. Designate the locomotor skill to be performed (e.g., taking giant steps) as well as the number of times to circle the play area. Choose a student to be the tagger. The tagger begins to try to tag other students. To avoid being tagged, students may find and touch with their toes the cards labeled with their own names. When a child is tagged, that child must circle the play area, performing the designated locomotor skill the specified number of times. After completing the movement, the child reenters the game. Remember to choose a new tagger often.

Word Tag

Equipment: word cards (make word cards from students' current reading program)

Task Analysis: muscular strength and endurance, cardiorespiratory endurance, language arts, letter sound recognition, visual memory, locomotor skills, figure-ground discrimination, form constancy, spatial-relationships, position in space, attention and concentration, hypotonic

Description: This tag game allows students to recognize and identify selected words. Begin by scattering the word cards throughout the play space. Designate the locomotor skill to be performed (e.g., hopping) as well as the number of times to circle the play area. Choose a student to be the tagger. Then, hold up a selected word card and say the word aloud. The tagger begins to try to tag other students. To avoid being tagged, students may find and touch with their toes a card with the selected word. When a child is tagged, that child must circle the play area, performing the designated locomotor skill the specified number of times. After completing the movement, the child reenters the game. Remember to choose a new tagger often.

Variation: A student can be safe from being tagged if that student repeats the selected word aloud.

Rhyming Tag

Equipment: selected rhyming word picture cards (found on pages 42–46)

Task Analysis: muscular strength and endurance, cardiorespiratory endurance, language arts, sound discrimination, rhyming words, visual memory, locomotor skills, figure-ground discrimination, form constancy, spatial relationships, position in space, attention and concentration, hypotonic

Description: This tag game allows students to recognize and identify selected rhyming words. Begin by scattering the rhyming word picture cards throughout the play space. Designate the locomotor skill to be performed (e.g., skating) as well as the number of times to circle the play area. Choose a student to be the tagger. Then, hold up a selected picture card and say the name of the picture aloud. The tagger begins to try to tag other students. To avoid being tagged, students may find and touch with their toes a picture whose name rhymes with the selected picture. When a child is tagged, that child must circle the play area, performing the designated locomotor skill the specified number of times. After completing the movement, the child reenters the game. Remember to choose a new tagger often.

(rhyming picture cards)

(train)   *(rain)*

(cat)

(hat)

(tree)

(bee)

(car)

(star)

(mice)

(dice)

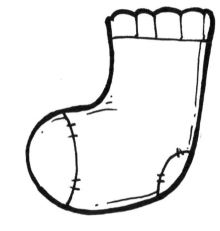

(sock)

(clock)

(can)

(fan)

(duck)

(truck)

(pig)

(wig)

(goat)

(boat)

(dog)

(frog)

(mitten)

(kitten)

(hen)

10

(ten)

Syllable Tag

Equipment: number cards (found on pages 53–56), word cards (make word cards from students' current reading program)

Task Analysis: arm strength, abdominal strength, muscular strength and endurance, cardiorespiratory endurance, bilateral activities, language arts, syllables, visual memory, locomotor skills, figure-ground discrimination, form constancy, spatial relationships, position in space, attention and concentration, hypotonic

Description: This tag game allows students to recognize and identify the number of syllables in a word. Begin by scattering the number cards throughout the play space. Designate the locomotor skill to be performed (e.g., stomping) or an animal walk (e.g., snake slither) as well as the number of times to circle the play area. Choose a student to be the tagger. Then, hold up a selected word card and say the word aloud. All of the children move through the play space performing the selected locomotor skill or animal walk. The tagger begins to try to tag other students. To avoid being tagged, students may find and touch with their toes a card with the number that is the number of syllables in the selected word. When a child is tagged, that child must circle the play area, performing a different locomotor skill the specified number of times. After completing the movement, the child reenters the game. Remember to choose a new tagger often.

Compound Word Tag

Equipment: compound word cards, each divided into the two separate words (compound word cards found on pages 48–50)

Task Analysis: arm strength, abdominal strength, muscular strength and endurance, cardiorespiratory endurance, bilateral activities, language arts, compound words, visual memory, locomotor skills, figure-ground discrimination, form constancy, spatial relationships, position in space, attention and concentration, hypotonic

straw / berry

dog \ house

Description: This tag game allows students to develop a vocabulary of compound words. Begin by scattering throughout the play space one word of each pair of words that join to make a compound word. Designate the locomotor skill to be performed (e.g., galloping) or an animal walk (e.g., caterpillar crawl) as well as the number of times to circle the play area. Choose a student to be the tagger. Then, hold up a word (e.g., cup) that is part of a compound word and say the word aloud. All of the children move through the play space performing the selected locomotor skill or animal walk. The tagger begins to try to tag other students. To avoid being tagged, students may find and touch with their toes a card with a word (e.g., cake) that combines with the selected word to make a compound word (e.g., cupcake). When a child is tagged, that child must circle the play area, performing a different locomotor skill the specified number of times. After completing the movement, the child reenters the game. Remember to choose a new tagger often.

Action Word Tag

Equipment: two sets of action word cards (action word cards found on pages 51-52)

Task Analysis: arm strength, abdominal strength, muscular strength and endurance, cardiorespiratory endurance, bilateral activities, locomotor skills, cognition, visual memory, visual discrimination, figure-ground discrimination, form constancy, spatial relationships, position in space, attention and concentration, hypotonic

Description: This tag game allows students to identify, recognize, and perform action words. Begin by scattering one set of action word cards throughout the play space. Designate the number of times a student who is tagged must circle the play area. Choose a student to be the tagger. Then, hold up a selected action word card and read it aloud. Students move through the play area performing this locomotor skill. The tagger begins to try to tag other students. To avoid being tagged, students may find and touch with their toes the action word card that matches the selected card and the action they are performing. When a child is tagged, that child must circle the play area, performing a different locomotor skill the specified number of times. After completing the movement, the child reenters the game. Remember to choose a new tagger often.

dog | house

rain | bow

snow | man

basket | ball

fire | fly

cup | cake

home	**sick**
straw	**berry**
tooth	**brush**
wheel	**chair**
turtle	**neck**
door	**bell**

lip stick

sail boat

finger nail

fire fighter

air plane

water fall

walk

jump

roll

wiggle

stomp

leap

crawl

tiptoe

twist

waddle

march

gallop

Math Tag Games

Number Tag

Equipment: number cards (found on pages 53–56)

Task Analysis: arm strength, abdominal strength, muscular strength and endurance, cardiorespiratory endurance, bilateral activities, mathematics, locomotor skills, figure-ground discrimination, form constancy, spatial relationships, position in space, attention and concentration, hypotonic

Description: This tag game allows students to recognize and identify numbers. Begin by scattering only the number cards throughout the play space. Designate the locomotor skill to be performed (e.g., walking backwards) or an animal walk (e.g., frog jump) as well as the number of times to circle the play area. Choose a student to be the tagger. Then, hold up a selected number card and say the number aloud. The tagger begins to try to tag other students. To avoid being tagged, students may find and touch with their toes the selected number card. When a child is tagged, that child must circle the play area, performing a different locomotor skill the specified number of times. After completing the movement, the child reenters the game. Remember to choose a new tagger often.

Variation: Instead of holding up a number card to begin the play, display a number word card. Students may then find the numeral that matches the number word.

Counting Tag

Equipment: number and sets of picture objects (found on pages 53–56)

Task Analysis: arm strength, abdominal strength, muscular strength and endurance, cardiorespiratory endurance, bilateral activities, mathematics, locomotor skills, figure-ground discrimination, form constancy, spatial relationships, position in space, attention and concentration, hypotonic

Description: This traditional tag game allows students to recognize and identify numbers. Begin by scattering the picture cards of sets of objects throughout the play space. Designate the locomotor skill to be performed (e.g., leaping) or an animal walk (e.g., mouse scurry) as well as the number of times to circle the play area. Choose a student to be the tagger. Then, hold up a selected number card and say the number aloud. The tagger begins to try to tag other students. To avoid being tagged, students may find and touch with their toes a picture card of a set with the same number of objects as the selected number. When a child is tagged, that child must circle the play area, performing a different locomotor skill the specified number of times. After completing the movement, the child reenters the game. Remember to choose a new tagger often.

Variation: Instead of holding up a number card to begin the play, display a number word card. Students may then find a picture of a set of objects that matches the number word.

(number and set cards)

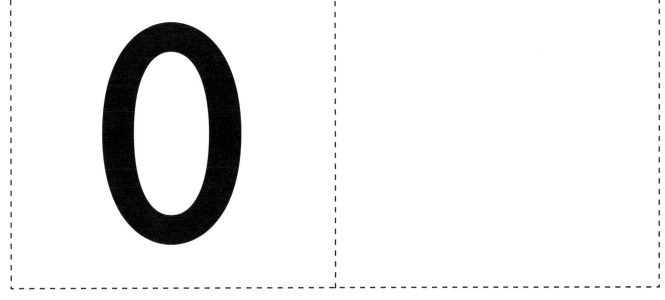

◆▼●■★◆▼●■★◆▼●■★◆▼●■★◆▼●■★◆▼●■★◆▼●■★◆▼●■★◆▼●■★◆▼

4

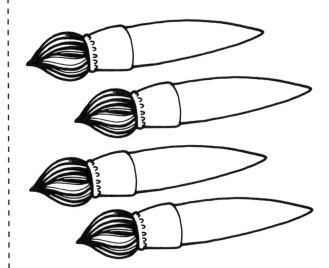

5

6

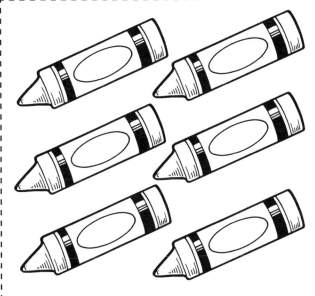

7

8

9

Number Jump Tag

Equipment: number cards (found on pages 53–56)

Task Analysis: arm strength, abdominal strength, muscular strength and endurance, cardiorespiratory endurance, bilateral activities, mathematics, locomotor skills, figure-ground discrimination, form constancy, spatial relationships, position in space, attention and concentration, visual motor coordination, hypotonic

Description: This tag game allows students to recognize, identify, and count numbers. Begin by scattering the number cards throughout the play space. Designate the locomotor skill to be performed (e.g., marching) or an animal walk (e.g., squirrel scamper) as well as the number of times to circle the play area. Choose a student to be the tagger.

Then, hold up a selected number card and say the number aloud. The tagger begins to try to tag other students. To avoid being tagged, students may find the cards with the selected number and jump up and down that many times. If a child is tagged before she completes the selected number of jumps, that child must circle the play area, performing a different locomotor skill the specified number of times. After completing the movement, the child reenters the game. Remember to choose a new tagger often.

Number Balance Tag

Equipment: number cards 1–4 (found on pages 54–55)

Task Analysis: arm strength, abdominal strength, muscular strength and endurance, cardiorespiratory endurance, bilateral activities, mathematics, crossing the midline, lateralization, body part awareness, static balance, visual memory, locomotor skills, figure-ground discrimination, form constancy, spatial relationships, position in space, attention and concentration, hypotonic

Description: This tag game allows students to recognize and count body parts. Designate the locomotor skill to be performed (e.g., hopping) or an animal walk (e.g., elephant walk) as well as the number of times to circle the play area. Choose a student to be the tagger. Then, hold up a selected number card and say the number aloud. The tagger begins to try to tag other students. To avoid being tagged, students may balance on the selected number of body parts (e.g., if the selected number is 3, a student may balance on two hands and one foot). If a child is tagged before balancing on the selected number of body parts, that child must circle the play area, performing a different locomotor skill the specified number of times. After completing the movement, the child reenters the game. Remember to choose a new tagger often.

Variation: Use numbers up to 15. This will challenge students to count fingers, elbows, knees, and so on, finding a variety of creative ways to balance on body parts.

Number Sentences Tag

Equipment: number cards (found on pages 53–56), math symbol cards (found on page 59)

Task Analysis: arm strength, abdominal strength, muscular strength and endurance, cardiorespiratory endurance, bilateral activities, mathematics, locomotor skills, figure-ground discrimination, form constancy, spatial relationships, position in space, attention and concentration, visual motor integration, hypotonic

Description: This tag game allows students to complete number sentences. Begin by scattering the flash cards throughout the play space. Designate the locomotor skill to be performed (e.g., skipping) or an animal walk (e.g., spider scuttle) as well as the number of times to circle the play area. Choose a student to be the tagger. Then, hold up a selected number card (e.g., 8) and say the number aloud. The tagger begins to try to tag other students. To avoid being tagged, students may find and touch with their toes the flash cards with numbers and operation equal to the selected number (e.g., 7 + 1, 2 + 6, 4 + 4, etc.). When a child is tagged, that child must circle the play area, performing a different locomotor skill the specified number of times. After completing the movement, the child reenters the game. Remember to choose a new tagger often.

Greater-Than, Less-Than Tag

Equipment: number cards (found on pages 53–56), greater-than and less-than symbol cards (found on page 58)

Task Analysis: arm strength, abdominal strength, muscular strength and endurance, cardiorespiratory endurance, bilateral activities, mathematics, locomotor skills, figure-ground discrimination, form constancy, spatial relationships, position in space, attention and concentration, hypotonic

Description: This tag game allows students to identify numbers that are greater-than or less-than a given number. Begin by scattering the number cards throughout the play space. Designate the locomotor skill to be performed (e.g., galloping) or an animal walk (e.g., duck waddle) as well as the number of times to circle the play area. Choose a student to be the tagger. Then, hold up a greater than or less than sign and a selected number card. Read the sign and number aloud (e.g., "greater-than 5"). The tagger begins to try to tag other students. To avoid being tagged, students may find and touch with their toes a number card that completes the number sentence correctly. When a child is tagged, that child must circle the play area, performing a different locomotor skill the specified number of times. After completing the movement, the child reenters the game. Remember to choose a new tagger often.

(greater-than, less-than symbol cards)

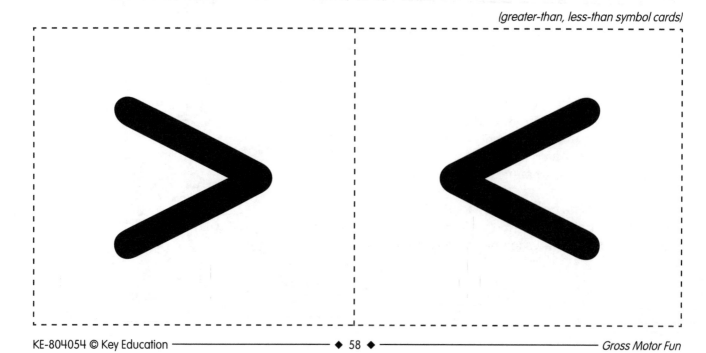

Addition and Subtraction Tag

Equipment: deck of playing cards, aces through 10s with no face cards; number cards (found on pages 53–56)

Task Analysis: arm strength, abdominal strength, muscular strength and endurance, cardiorespiratory endurance, bilateral activities, mathematics, locomotor skills, form constancy, spatial relationships, position in space, visual memory, attention and concentration, hypotonic

Description: This tag game allows students to work together to create number sentences. Designate the locomotor skill to be performed (e.g., skating) or an animal walk (e.g., kangaroo hop) as well as the number of times to circle the play area. Choose a student to be the tagger and provide every child with a number card. Then, hold up a selected number card and say the number aloud. The tagger begins to try to tag other students. To avoid being tagged, each student may find and stand next to another student whose number, when added to or subtracted from the student's number, equals the selected number (e.g., if the selected number is 8, students may work together to create 3 + 5, 9 – 1, 6 + 2, etc.). If a child is tagged before creating a number sentence with another student, that child must circle the play area, performing a different locomotor skill the specified number of times. After completing the movement, the child reenters the game. Remember to choose a new tagger often.

(math symbol cards)

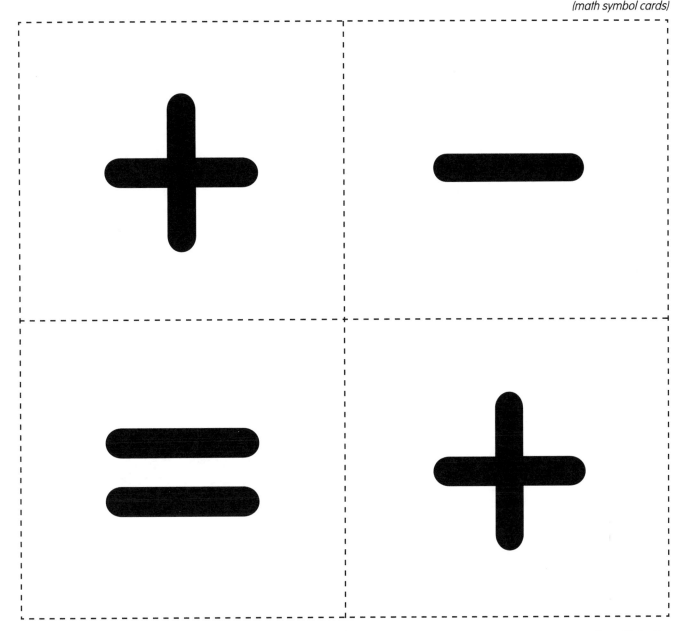

Chapter 2: Remember Hopscotch?

Traditionally, hopscotch is a playground game children play at recess. However, hopscotch can be incorporated into your school day to support academic concepts both inside and outside the classroom. When played outside, many different innovative and creative hopscotch patterns can be drawn. Patterns created with sidewalk chalk on playgrounds give flexibility to originate different challenges for children, based on their developmental profiles. When playing inside, masking tape can be used on floors to create similar challenges.

Hopscotch affords each student opportunities to develop gross body coordination, static and dynamic balance, eye-foot coordination, eye-foot accuracy, and eye-hand accuracy. Visual motor coordination, lateralization, crossing the midline, visual motor integration, figure-ground discrimination, spatial relationships, and position in space are also addressed as children engage in hopscotch-based activities. Using a variety of different objects and/or pictures to play allows students to develop form discrimination, visual discrimination, and visual memory skills. The health-related fitness skills of explosive leg power, muscular strength, and muscular endurance build up strong bodies and, as an added benefit, strong minds. With increased strength and endurance, students can sit in their chairs for longer periods and give greater attention to the tasks presented to them without fatiguing.

Use your imagination, as well as the ideas of your students, to create some very interesting and nontraditional hopscotch patterns. The size and length of the hopscotch pattern should match the developmental levels of your students. Then, you can provide academic challenges within the curriculum guidelines that match the cognitive abilities of your students.

Hopping and jumping into spaces enhances a child's understanding of laterality that is used in reading; the ability to perform bilateral tasks, such as stabilizing the paper with the nondominant hand when writing; and to grasp directionality concepts used in spacing words and letters on paper. As children practice using both the right and left sides of their bodies and their laterality develops, the possibility of problems with reversals is reduced. As noted earlier, gross motor development precedes fine motor. As children achieve greater control of their bodies during these hopscotch games, this control will contribute to the development of fine motor control in desktop activities such as writing, coloring, and cutting.

All of the hopscotch games included in this chapter should be played in a noncompetitive manner, with no elimination; all children should have the opportunity to enjoy the game. Allow children to choose what types of objects they want to toss to serve as markers (for example, a small rock for an outside game, or a beanbag for an inside game). Many of the following games can also be played using flash cards, a spinner (pattern found on page 63) or a rolling cube (pattern found on page 62) which can be easily adapted for the particular skill that you wish to teach. Construct the spinner or rolling cube according to the directions on the pattern pages. The spinner and rolling cube can be labeled with the appropriate letters, numbers, words, shapes, or other specific game content. The student gently rolls the cube; when the cube stops, the letter, number, etc., that is facing up is selected. See page 61 for hopscotch examples and directions.

Sample Hopscotch Grids

Directions:

1. Use outlines of animal shapes to develop the spaces, in either single or double formations.

2. Make different sizes of grids, such as 6' x 6' (1.8 m x 1.8 m), 10' x 10' (3 m x 3 m), and so on, to include the information on which you are working.

3. Create outlines of trees, leaves, acorns, etc.

4. Draw outlines around the children themselves!

5. Use outlines of geometric shapes. Then, if you wish to expand upon this idea, create the inside grids of the patterns with more of the same shapes (e.g., if using the outline of a triangle, all of the shapes inside the outline should also be triangles).

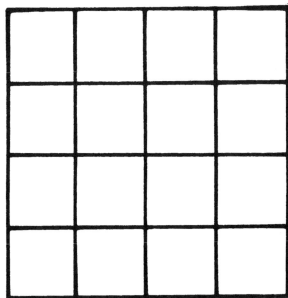

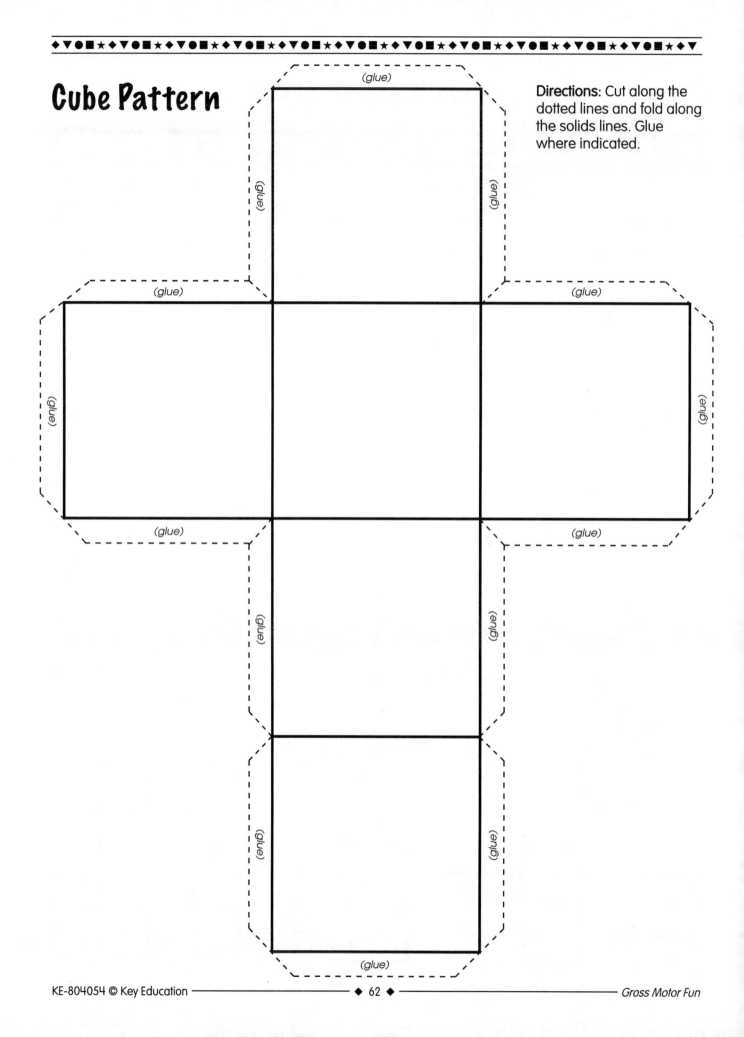

Cube Pattern

Directions: Cut along the dotted lines and fold along the solids lines. Glue where indicated.

(glue)

(glue)

(glue)

(glue)

(glue)

(glue)

(glue)

(glue)

(glue)

(glue)

(glue)

(glue)

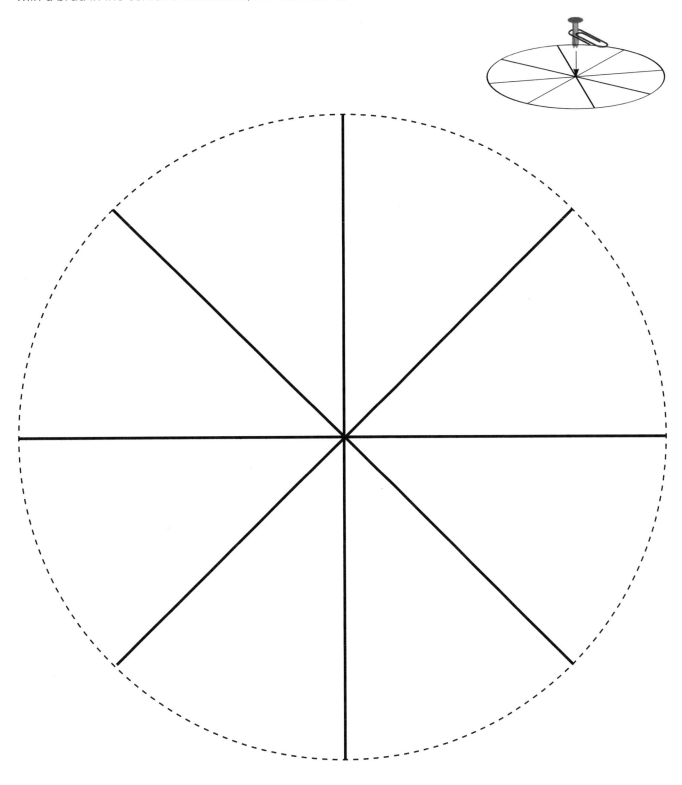

Spinner Pattern

Directions: Copy the spinner pattern on card stock and cut out along the dotted lines. Attach a paper clip with a brad in the center of the circle. *(See illustration.)*

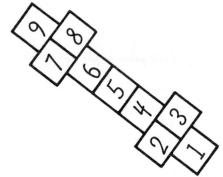

Traditional Hopscotch

Equipment: marker (e.g., small rock, beanbag) to toss; sidewalk chalk or masking tape

Task Analysis: muscular strength and endurance, cardiorespiratory endurance, bilateral activities, dynamic balance, body part awareness, static balance, visual memory, locomotor skills, explosive leg power, number sequencing, eye-foot accuracy, crossing the midline, visual motor coordination, attention and concentration, number recognition

Description: Play a traditional hopscotch game using a pattern with a size and length that matches your students' abilities. Have the first student toss the marker into space number 1. The student then hops over space 1 and continues to the end of the pattern, hopping on one foot in a single space and jumping on both feet—one in each space—when two spaces are side by side. When the end of the pattern is reached, the student turns around and hops back, stopping in space 2 to balance on one foot while picking up the marker in space 1. The student then hops in space 1 and out of the pattern. That student then continues the turn by tossing the marker into space 2 and so on. The student never hops in the same space that contains the marker. If a student's marker misses the correct space, or the student loses balance, or steps on a line, it is the next student's turn. Students should resume their turns where they left off. Play continues until all children have had an opportunity to reach the highest number on the pattern.

Early Learning Hopscotch Games

Matching Colors Hopscotch

Equipment: color cards, color spinner (pattern found on page 63) or a color rolling cube (pattern found on page 62); sidewalk chalk or masking tape; marker (e.g., small rock, beanbag) to toss

Task Analysis: muscular strength and endurance, cardiorespiratory endurance, bilateral activities, dynamic balance, body part awareness, static balance, visual memory, visual discrimination, locomotor skills, explosive leg power, color identification, eye-foot accuracy, crossing the midline, visual motor coordination, attention and concentration, figure-ground discrimination, form constancy, spatial relationships, position in space

Description: Create a hopscotch pattern. Place a color card in each space; each color should be included several times. To select a color, have the first student either use the color spinner, draw a color card, or gently roll the cube (the color on the top face of the cube is the selected color to find). The student should scan the hopscotch pattern for the selected color and then begin to hop on that color from space to space until returning to the starting space. The next student selects a new color to find. Specific color searches can also be repeated for reinforcement.

Variations: 1. The student may toss a marker into each space containing the selected color before hopping into it.

2. Instead of placing color cards on the hopscotch pattern, write a color word in each space; each color word should be included several times. Students will find the color words for each selected color.

3. Use color words on the spinner or cube or color word flash cards to select the color students must find.

Picture Identification Hopscotch

Equipment: sets of picture cards, spinner with pictures (pattern found on page 63) or rolling cube (pattern found on page 62); sidewalk chalk or masking tape; marker (e.g., small rock, beanbag) to toss

Task Analysis: muscular strength and endurance, cardiorespiratory endurance, bilateral activities, dynamic balance, body part awareness, static balance, visual memory, visual discrimination, locomotor skills, explosive leg power, picture identification, eye-foot accuracy, crossing the midline, visual motor coordination, attention and concentration, figure-ground discrimination, form constancy, spatial relationships, position in space

Description: Create a hopscotch pattern. In each space, place a picture card; each picture should be included several times. To select a picture, have the first student either use the spinner, draw a picture card, or gently roll the cube (the picture on the top face of the cube is the selected picture to find). The student should scan the hopscotch pattern for the selected picture and then begin to hop on that picture from space to space until returning to the starting space. The next student selects a new picture to find. Specific picture searches can also be repeated for reinforcement.

Variation: The student may toss a marker into each space containing the selected picture before hopping into it.

Matching Shapes Hopscotch

Equipment: shape cutouts, or a spinner (pattern found on page 63), or rolling cube (pattern found on page 62); sidewalk chalk or masking tape; marker (e.g., small rock, beanbag) to toss

Task Analysis: muscular strength and endurance, cardiorespiratory endurance, bilateral activities, dynamic balance, body part awareness, static balance, visual memory, visual discrimination, locomotor skills, explosive leg power, geometric shape identification, eye-foot accuracy, crossing the midline, visual motor coordination, attention and concentration, figure-ground discrimination, form constancy, spatial relationships, position in space

Description: Create a hopscotch pattern. In each space, draw a geometric shape; each shape should be included several times. To select a shape, have the first student either use the shape spinner, draw a shape card, or gently roll the cube (the shape on the top face of the cube is the selected shape to find). The student should scan the hopscotch pattern for the selected shape and then begin to hop on that shape from space to space until returning to the starting space. The next student selects a new shape to find. Specific shape searches can also be repeated for reinforcement.

Variations: I. The student may toss a marker into each space containing the selected shape before hopping into it.

2. On the spinner, shape cards, or rolling cube, use a variety of shapes in various colors. This will challenge the students to focus on one attribute (shape) even when it is presented in a variety of colors.

What's Missing? Hopscotch

Equipment: flash cards depicting sequences (e.g., numbers, letters, shapes) that students are learning, making sure each sequence is missing one element; sidewalk chalk or masking tape; marker (e.g., small rock, beanbag) to toss

Task Analysis: muscular strength and endurance, cardiorespiratory endurance, bilateral activities, dynamic balance, body part awareness, static balance, visual memory, visual discrimination, locomotor skills, explosive leg power, cognition, word recognition, number recognition, shape recognition, form discrimination, visual closure, eye-foot accuracy, crossing the midline, visual motor coordination, attention and concentration, figure-ground discrimination, form constancy, spatial relationships, position in space

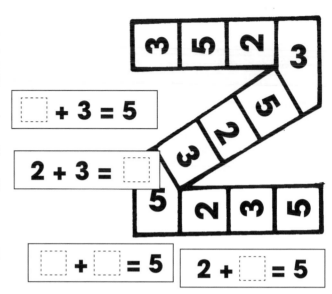

Description: Create a hopscotch pattern. In each space, write a number, letter, or draw a shape that completes the sequences on the flash cards. Each element should be shown several times. Use the flash cards to have a student select a sequence to complete. The student should scan the hopscotch pattern for the missing element and then begin to hop on the correct answer from space to space until returning to the starting space. The next student selects a new sequence to complete. Specific sequences can also be repeated for reinforcement.

Variation: The student may toss a marker into each space containing the missing element before hopping into it.

Street Sign Hopscotch

Equipment: sets of street sign picture cards, spinner (pattern found on page 63) or rolling cube (pattern found on page 62) with pictures of street signs; sidewalk chalk or masking tape; marker (e.g., small rock, beanbag) to toss

Task Analysis: muscular strength and endurance, cardiorespiratory endurance, bilateral activities, dynamic balance, body part awareness, static balance, visual memory, visual discrimination, locomotor skills, explosive leg power, cognition, word recognition, safety, eye-foot accuracy, crossing the midline, visual motor coordination, attention and concentration, figure-ground discrimination, form constancy, spatial relationships, position in space

Description: Create a hopscotch pattern. In each space, place a street sign picture card; each sign should be included several times. To select a street sign, have the first student use either the spinner, draw a street sign picture card, or gently roll the cube (the street sign on the top face of the cube is the selected sign to find). The student should scan the hopscotch pattern for the selected street sign and then begin to hop on that sign from space to space until returning to the starting space. The next student selects a new street sign picture to find. Specific street sign searches can also be repeated for reinforcement. This game is a great way to review information that has been taught, prepare for a quiz, or pretest students' knowledge when presenting new material.

Variation: The student may toss a marker into each space containing the selected street sign before hopping into it.

Language Arts Hopscotch Games

Rhyming Hopscotch

Equipment: word family flash cards, spinner (pattern found on page 63), or rolling cube (pattern found on page 62) labeled with words from several word families; sidewalk chalk or masking tape; marker (e.g., small rock, beanbag) to toss

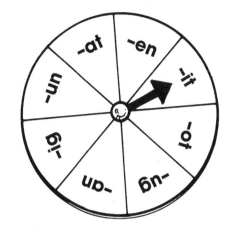

Task Analysis: muscular strength and endurance, cardiorespiratory endurance, bilateral activities, dynamic balance, body part awareness, static balance, visual memory, visual discrimination, locomotor skills, explosive leg power, rhyming words and sounds, eye-foot accuracy, crossing the midline, visual motor coordination, attention and concentration, figure-ground discrimination, form constancy, spatial relationships, position in space

Description: Create a hopscotch pattern. In each space, write a rhyming word from the word families featured on the spinner, flash cards, or rolling cube. Include several words from each word family. To select a rhyming word, have the first student use either the spinner, draw a flash card, or gently roll the cube (the word family word on the top face of the cube is the selected rhyme to find). The student should scan the hopscotch pattern for words from the selected word family and then begin to hop on the rhyming words from space to space until returning to the starting space. The next student selects a new rhyming word to find. Specific word family searches can also be repeated for reinforcement.

Variation: The student may toss a marker into each space containing a rhyming word before hopping into it.

Letter Hopscotch

Equipment: spinner (pattern found on page 63), letter flash cards, or rolling cube (pattern found on page 62) labeled with letters; sidewalk chalk or masking tape; marker (e.g., small rock, beanbag) to toss

Task Analysis: muscular strength and endurance, cardiorespiratory endurance, bilateral activities, dynamic balance, body part awareness, static balance, visual memory, visual discrimination, locomotor skills, explosive leg power, letter identification, eye-foot accuracy, crossing the midline, visual motor coordination, attention and concentration

Description: Create a hopscotch pattern. In each space, write a letter students are learning to identify; each letter should be written several times. To select a letter, have the first student use either the letter spinner, draw a flash card, or gently roll the letter cube (the letter on the top face of the cube is the selected letter to find). The student should scan the hopscotch pattern for the selected letter and then begin to hop on the letter from space to space until returning to the starting space. The next student selects a new letter to find. Specific letter searches can also be repeated for reinforcement.

Variation: The student may toss a marker into each space containing the selected letter before hopping into it.

Vowel/Consonant Hopscotch

Equipment: spinner (pattern found on page 63) labeled with the words *vowel* and *consonant;* sidewalk chalk or masking tape; marker (e.g., small rock, beanbag) to toss

Task Analysis: muscular strength and endurance, cardiorespiratory endurance, bilateral activities, dynamic balance, body part awareness, static balance, visual memory, visual discrimination, locomotor skills, explosive leg power, vowel/consonant recognition, eye-foot accuracy, crossing the midline, visual motor coordination, attention and concentration, figure-ground discrimination, form constancy, spatial relationships, position in space

Description: Create a hopscotch pattern. In each space, write either a vowel or a consonant, making sure to have a variety of each. Have the first student use the spinner to select which type of letter she will find. The student should scan the hopscotch pattern for the selected type of letter—a vowel or a consonant—and then begin to hop on the selected letters from space to space until returning to the starting space. The next student spins again to select the type of letter to find. Specific vowel or consonant searches can also be repeated for reinforcement.

Variations: I. The student may toss a marker into each space containing the type of letter selected by the spinner before hopping into it.

2. The student may toss a marker onto the hopscotch pattern. He must then call out the word *vowel* or *consonant* to name the type of letter before hopping into the space. Repeat.

Blended Sounds Hopscotch

Equipment: letter blend flash cards, spinner (pattern found on page 63), or rolling cube (pattern found on page 62) labeled with letter blends; sidewalk chalk or masking tape; marker (e.g., small rock, beanbag) to toss

Task Analysis: muscular strength and endurance, cardiorespiratory endurance, bilateral activities, dynamic balance, body part awareness, static balance, visual memory, visual discrimination, locomotor skills, explosive leg power, blended sounds identification, eye-foot accuracy, crossing the midline, visual motor coordination, attention and concentration, figure-ground discrimination, form constancy, spatial relationships, position in space

Description: Create a hopscotch pattern. In each space, write a blended sound students are learning to identify; each letter blend should be written several times. To select a blended sound, have the first student use either the letter blends spinner, letter blends flash cards, or gently roll the cube (the letter blend on the top face of the cube is the selected blend to find). The student should scan the hopscotch pattern for the selected blended sound and then begin to hop on the blend from space to space until returning to the starting space. The next student selects a new blended sound to find. Specific letter blend searches can also be repeated for reinforcement.

Variation: The student may toss a marker into each space containing the selected blended sound before hopping into it.

Spelling Hopscotch

Equipment: spelling word cards, spinner (pattern found on page 63), or rolling cube (pattern found on page 62) with spelling words; sidewalk chalk or masking tape; marker (e.g., small rock, beanbag) to toss

Task Analysis: muscular strength and endurance, cardiorespiratory endurance, bilateral activities, dynamic balance, body part awareness, static balance, visual memory, visual discrimination, locomotor skills, explosive leg power, spelling words, eye-foot accuracy, crossing the midline, visual motor coordination, attention and concentration, figure-ground discrimination, form constancy, spatial relationships, position in space

Description: Create a hopscotch pattern. In each space, write a spelling word with a missing letter or letters, e.g., *m_rching, mar_h_ng, (marching); _eaping, lea_ing, (leaping); e_ting, ea_ing, (eating);* etc. You may segment each spelling word in as many ways as you feel are appropriate. To select a spelling word, have the first student use either the spinner, draw a word card, or gently roll the cube (the spelling word on the top face of the cube is the selected word to find). The student should scan the hopscotch pattern for the matching spelling word with the missing letters, and then begin to hop on the spelling words from space to space until returning to the starting space. The next student selects a new spelling word to find. Specific spelling word searches can also be repeated for reinforcement.

Variations: The student may toss a marker into each space containing a spelling word before hopping into it. Have the student spell the word, including the missing letter or letters, in each spelling word as she hops into the space.

Word Wall Hopscotch

Equipment: spinner (pattern found on page 63), word wall word flash cards, or rolling cube (pattern found on page 62) labeled with word wall words; sidewalk chalk or masking tape; marker (e.g., small rock, beanbag) to toss

Task Analysis: muscular strength and endurance, cardiorespiratory endurance, bilateral activities, dynamic balance, body part awareness, static balance, visual memory, visual discrimination, locomotor skills, explosive leg power, word identification, eye-foot accuracy, crossing the midline, visual motor coordination, attention and concentration, figure-ground discrimination, form constancy, spatial relationships, position in space

Description: Create a hopscotch pattern. In each space, write a word wall word students are learning to identify; each word should be written several times. To select a word wall word, have the first student use either the letter spinner, draw a flash card, or gently roll the cube (the word wall word on the top face of the cube is the selected word to find). The student should scan the hopscotch pattern for the selected word wall word and then begin to hop on the word from space to space until returning to the starting space. The next student selects a new word wall word to find. Specific word searches can also be repeated for reinforcement.

Variation: The student may toss a marker into each space containing the selected word wall word before hopping into it.

Sight Word Sentence Hopscotch

Equipment: flash cards with simple sentences that use many of the same words (e.g., I did see the bird. He did see the car. I did not hear the bird.); sidewalk chalk or masking tape; marker (e.g., small rock, beanbag) to toss

Task Analysis: muscular strength and endurance, cardiorespiratory endurance, bilateral activities, dynamic balance, body part awareness, static balance, visual memory, visual discrimination, locomotor skills, explosive leg power, cognition, word recognition, sentence structure, eye-foot accuracy, crossing the midline, visual motor coordination, attention and concentration, figure-ground discrimination, form constancy, spatial relationships, position in space

Description: Create a hopscotch pattern. In each space, write one of a variety of words that can be combined to form the sentences on the flash cards. Use the flash cards to have a student select a sentence to complete. The student should scan the hopscotch pattern for the correct order of the words in the selected sentence and then begin to hop on the words in order from space to space. The next student selects a new sentence to complete. Specific sentences can also be repeated for reinforcement.

Variations: 1. The student may toss a marker into each space containing the next word in the sentence before hopping into it.

2. Allow students to create their own sentences by hopping from word to word in the hopscotch pattern.

I	look	see	the
and	can	jump	at
play	the	dog	run
cat	a	with	bird

Look at the dog.

I see a bird.

Look at the cat play.

The cat and dog run.

The dog can jump.

I can see the bird.

I can play with the dog and the cat.

The dog and the cat see the bird.

Math Hopscotch Games

Counting Hopscotch

Equipment: sets of objects cards (found on pages 53–56), spinner (pattern found on page 63), or rolling cube (pattern found on page 62) with pictures of sets of objects (e.g., picture of nine ducks); sidewalk chalk or masking tape; marker (e.g., small rock, beanbag) to toss

Task Analysis: muscular strength and endurance, cardiorespiratory endurance, bilateral activities, dynamic balance, body part awareness, static balance, visual memory, visual discrimination, locomotor skills, explosive leg power, mathematics, number recognition, eye-foot accuracy, crossing the midline, visual motor coordination, attention and concentration, figure-ground discrimination, form constancy, spatial relationships, position in space

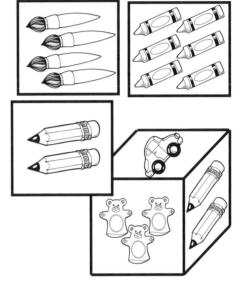

Description: Create a hopscotch pattern. In each space, write a number to which students are learning to count; each number should be written several times. To select a set of objects, have the first student use either the spinner, draw a card with a picture of a set of objects, or gently roll the cube (the set of objects on the top face of the cube is the selected set to count). The student should scan the hopscotch pattern for the number of the objects in the set and then begin to hop on the numbers from space to space until returning to the starting space. The next student selects a new set of objects to count. Specific searches for numbers of objects can also be repeated for reinforcement.

Variation: The student may toss a marker into each space containing the number of objects in the set before hopping into it.

Number Hopscotch

Equipment: number cards (found on pages 53–56), spinner (pattern found on page 63) or rolling cube (pattern found on page 62); sidewalk chalk or masking tape; marker (e.g., small rock, beanbag) to toss

Task Analysis: muscular strength and endurance, cardiorespiratory endurance, bilateral activities, dynamic balance, body part awareness, static balance, visual memory, visual discrimination, locomotor skills, explosive leg power, number identification, eye-foot accuracy, crossing the midline, visual motor coordination, attention and concentration, figure-ground discrimination, form constancy, spatial relationships, position in space

Description: Create a hopscotch pattern. In each space, write a number students are learning to identify; each number should be written several times. To select a number, have the first student use either the number spinner, draw a number card, or gently roll the number cube (the number on the top face of the cube is the selected number to find). The student should scan the hopscotch pattern for the selected number and then begin to hop on the number from space to space until returning to the starting space. The next student selects a new number to find. Specific number searches can also be repeated for reinforcement.

Variation: The student may toss a marker into each space containing the selected number before hopping into it.

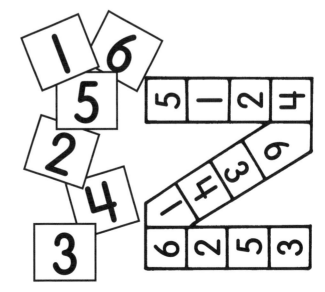

Number Sentence Hopscotch

Equipment: number cards (found on pages 53–56), spinner (pattern found on page 63), or rolling cube (pattern found on page 62); sidewalk chalk or masking tape; marker (e.g., small rock, beanbag) to toss

Task Analysis: muscular strength and endurance, cardiorespiratory endurance; bilateral activities, dynamic balance, body part awareness, static balance, visual memory, visual discrimination, locomotor skills, explosive leg power, number sentence identification (addition, subtraction, division, and multiplication facts), eye-foot accuracy, crossing the midline, visual motor coordination, attention and concentration, figure-ground discrimination, form constancy, spatial relationships, position in space

Description: Create a hopscotch pattern. In each space, write numbers and an operation students are learning to solve; several sets of numbers and operations (e.g., 7 + 1, 2 + 6, 4 + 4, 5 + 3—should equal the same number). To select a number, have the first student use either the number spinner, draw a number card, or gently roll the number cube (the number on the top face of the cube is the selected number to find). The student should scan the hopscotch pattern for the numbers and operations that equal the selected number and then begin to hop on the numbers and operations from space to space until returning to the starting space. The next student selects a new number to find. Specific number searches can also be repeated for reinforcement.

Variation: The student may toss a marker into each space containing the numbers and operation that equal the selected number before hopping into it.

Coin Recognition Hopscotch

Equipment: money cards (found on pages 73–74), spinner (pattern found on page 63), or rolling cube (pattern found on page 62) picturing single coins—penny, nickle, dime, quarter, and half-dollar; sidewalk chalk or masking tape; marker (e.g., small rock, beanbag) to toss

Task Analysis: muscular strength and endurance, cardiorespiratory endurance, bilateral activities, dynamic balance, body part awareness, static balance, visual memory, visual discrimination, locomotor skills, explosive leg power, cognition, math skills, word recognition, eye-foot accuracy, crossing the midline, visual motor coordination, attention and concentration, figure-ground discrimination, form constancy, spatial relationships, position in space

Description: Create a hopscotch pattern. In each space, write one of a variety of coin descriptions students are learning to identify (more than one type of coin should be included). Describe the coins in four ways (e.g., penny, one cent, $0.01, 1¢.) To select a coin, have the first student use the spinner, draw a coin, or gently roll the cube (the coin on the top face of the cube is the selected coin to find). The student should scan the hopscotch pattern for different ways the coin can be expressed and then begin to hop on the coin descriptions from space to space until returning to the starting space. The next student selects a new coin to find. Specific coin searches can also be repeated for reinforcement. This game is a great way to review information that has been taught, prepare for a quiz, or pretest students' knowledge when presenting new material.

Variations: The student may toss a marker into each space containing descriptions of the selected coin before hopping into it. As a student jumps from one coin description to the next, she may add the amounts and call out each number to practice counting on by 1s, 5s, 10s, and 25s.

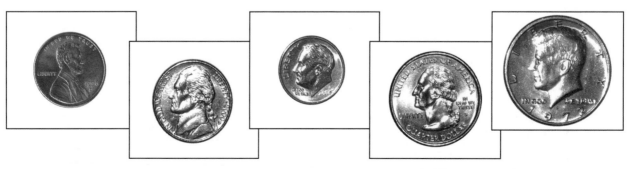

Money Hopscotch

Equipment: Money word cards indicating monetary denominations students are learning (e.g., six dollars, six dollars and fifty cents, six dollars and twenty-five cents), spinner (pattern found on page 63) or rolling cube (pattern found on page 62); single coin and bill cards (found on pages 73–74); sidewalk chalk or masking tape; marker (e.g., small rock, beanbag) to toss

Task Analysis: muscular strength and endurance, cardiorespiratory endurance, bilateral activities, dynamic balance, body part awareness, static balance, visual memory, visual discrimination, locomotor skills, explosive leg power, money awareness and recognition, eye-foot accuracy, crossing the midline, visual motor coordination, attention and concentration, figure-ground discrimination, form constancy, spatial relationships, position in space

Description: Create a hopscotch pattern. In each space, write a monetary denomination that students are learning in numeral form. Repeat each monetary amount several places on the pattern. To select a money word, have the first student use either the spinner, draw a money word card, or gently roll the cube (the money word on the top face of the cube is the selected monetary amount.

The student should scan the hopscotch pattern for the numerals that show the same amount as the selected money word. The student should then begin to hop on the numerals from space to space until returning to the starting space. The next student selects a new money word. Specific money searches can also be repeated for reinforcement.

Variations: 1. The student may toss a marker into each space containing the money numerals before hopping into it.

2. Instead of writing monetary amounts in numeral form on the hopscotch pattern, show the amount with drawings of coins and bills. Continue as described above.

(money cards)

Chapter 3: Academic Relays

Relays are lots of fun for children. Relays provide a form of controlled competition, and it is always exciting to try to finish first in a relay! Other benefits of relay games are obvious as children learn how to take turns, feel part of a group, practice sportsmanship, and gain understanding of others' abilities.

A vast variety of gross motor skills can be included when developing relay themes. Your imagination is only limited by what you choose to include in a relay. In addition to the specific benefits of strong gross motor development, these skills provide the proper foundation of upper body musculature, core strength, and endurance, which all contribute to fine motor development.

Relays also provide students a fantastic way to practice fine motor skills while including academic concepts. As you engage students in the curriculum, relays can provide numerous physical challenges for small muscle movements. For example, developing graphomotor skills is critical, especially in the primary grades where students are required to hold pencils and "write across the curriculum."

Academic relays allow classroom teachers to complement the curriculum of the physical education teacher. In return, the physical education teacher can provide gross motor skill developmental activities that also complement the classroom's curriculum by adding a number of themes to the relays based on the academic content being learned in the classroom.

Most young children are physical learners. However, others may be either tactile learners, needing to touch and feel objects as they explore and learn, or kinesthetic and proprioceptive learners, who need to move the large muscles of the body as they send signals to the motor areas of the brain. Using the kinesthetic modality through movement and throughout the environment enhances learning experiences. Academic relays meet the needs of both tactile and kinesthetic learners.

A few suggestions to keep in mind as you plan your relays:
- The distances between the relay lines and the designated "turn around" area will depend on the developmental level of your students. The longer the distance, the greater the challenge will be in the area of muscular strength and endurance.
- When dividing the class into teams or small groups, remember that the smaller the group, the more movement (and the less sitting) that will take place.
- Adapt the chosen relay to the play space available, whether the classroom, the gymnasium, or outside.
- If the relay has specific tasks that will be done in order, be sure to mix up the order of the students in line when repeating the activity so that students will face different challenges.
- During these fun relays, students' abilities to think fast will be stimulated and challenged. Shift the focus from the competitiveness of the relay by de-emphasizing the aspects of winning and losing.
- Academic relays can stimulate major areas of development, such as gross motor skills, fine motor skills, cognitive skills, and social and emotional development. Add these benefits to your students' growth in a most enjoyable way!

Movement and Gross Motor Relay Games

Locomotor Relay
Equipment: none
Task Analysis: muscular strength and endurance, cardiorespiratory endurance, bilateral activities, dynamic balance, body part awareness, static balance, locomotor skills, explosive leg power, hypotonic

Description: Divide the class into small groups of four to six students. Choose a locomotor skill (e.g., skipping). Have the first students in line perform the locomotor skill to a designated spot and then return to their lines. The next student in each line will then perform the skill and the relay continues until all students have completed the task. Other suggested locomotor movements include: crawling, creeping, galloping, hopping, jumping, leaping, marching, rolling, running, sliding, and walking.

Animal Walk Relay

Equipment: none

Task Analysis: muscular strength and endurance, cardiorespiratory endurance, bilateral activities, dynamic balance, body part awareness, static balance, locomotor skills, explosive leg power, upper body muscular strength, hypotonic, lateralization, crossing the midline

Description: Divide the class into small groups of four to six students. Choose an animal walk (e.g., bear walk). Have the first students in line perform the animal walk to a designated spot and then return to their lines. The next student in each line will then perform the walk and the relay continues until all students have completed the task. Other suggested animal walk movements include: frogleap, crab, duck waddle, elephant walk, inchworm inch, bunny hop, horse gallop, and seal slide.

Dynamic Balance Relay

Equipment: beams, stepping stones, jump ropes, masking tape

Task Analysis: muscular strength and endurance, cardiorespiratory endurance, bilateral activities, dynamic balance, body part awareness, locomotor skills, explosive leg power, hypotonic, eye-foot accuracy, lateralization, crossing the midline, visual motor integration

Description: Design a course of balance skill challenges based on the developmental level of students. For example, if you want students to walk on a line, one-inch-wide masking tape may require a level of balance much more precise than if you made a course with two parallel lines of masking tape three to four inches apart, allowing students to step in between the lines of tape.

Divide the class into small groups of four to six students. Have the first students in line move through the activity area using dynamic balancing skills (e.g., stepping on a layout of jump ropes, between lines of masking tape) to a designated spot and then return to their lines. The next student in each line will then perform the skill and the relay continues until all students have completed the task.

Bounce and Catch Relay

Equipment: balls of different sizes (decreasing the size of the balls increases the level of skill needed to complete the task)

Task Analysis: muscular strength and endurance, cardiorespiratory endurance, bilateral activities, dynamic balance, body part awareness, static balance, eye-hand coordination, eye-hand accuracy, locomotor skills, explosive leg power, visual motor coordination, attention and concentration

Description: Divide the class into small groups of four to six students. Have the first student in each line bounce and catch a ball while moving forward to a designated spot and then return to the line, handing off the ball to the next student. The next student will then perform the skill and the relay continues until all students have completed the task.

Variation: Add to the challenge by selecting a locomotor movement for students to perform as they move.

Toss and Catch Relay

Equipment: scarves, beanbags, or balls in different sizes (decreasing the size of the objects increases the level of skill needed to complete the task)

Task Analysis: muscular strength and endurance, cardiorespiratory endurance, bilateral activities, dynamic balance, body part awareness, static balance, eye-hand coordination, eye-hand accuracy, locomotor skills, explosive leg power, visual tracking skills, visual motor coordination, attention and concentration

Description: Choose objects for the students to toss and catch based on their developmental level and the skills you wish to address. Divide the class into small groups of four to six students. Have the first students in line toss up and catch the objects while moving forward to a designated spot and then return to their lines, handing off the objects to the next students in line. The next students will then perform the skill and the relay continues until all students have completed the task.

Variation: Add to the challenge by selecting a locomotor movement for students to perform as they move.

Balloon Relay

Equipment: balloons in different sizes (decreasing the size of the balloons increases the level of skill needed to complete the task)

Task Analysis: muscular strength and endurance, cardiorespiratory endurance, bilateral activities, dynamic balance, body part awareness, eye-hand coordination, eye-hand accuracy, locomotor skills, explosive leg power, visual tracking skills, visual motor coordination, crossing the midline, attention and concentration, lateralization

Description: Divide the class into small groups of four to six students. Have the first students in line tap the balloons to keep them aloft while moving forward to a designated spot and then return to their lines, handing off the balloons to the next students in line. The next students will then perform the skill and the relay continues until all students have completed the task.

Variation: Add to the challenge by selecting a locomotor movement for students to perform as they move.

Throwing Relay

Equipment: beanbags in different sizes, targets (such as hoops), masking tape outlines on the floor or wall (decreasing the size of the targets increases the level of skill needed to complete the task)

Task Analysis: muscular strength and endurance, cardiorespiratory endurance, bilateral activities, dynamic balance, body part awareness, eye-hand coordination, eye-hand accuracy, locomotor skills, explosive leg power, visual tracking skills, visual motor coordination

Description: Divide the class into small groups of four to six students. Choose a locomotor skill (e.g., jumping) or an animal walk (e.g., crab scuttle). Have the first students in line perform the locomotor skill or animal walk to a designated spot, pick up a beanbag, toss it into a target, and then return to their lines. If the student misses the target, he may try again before returning to the line. The next student in each line will then perform the skill and the relay continues until all students have completed the task.

Stepping Stones Relay

Equipment: floor markers in a variety of different sizes, colors, or shapes

Task Analysis: motor planning, muscular strength and endurance, cardiorespiratory endurance, bilateral activities, dynamic balance, body part awareness, eye-foot coordination, eye-foot accuracy, locomotor skills, explosive leg power, visual tracking skills, visual memory, crossing the midline, visual motor coordination, attention and concentration, figure-ground discrimination, form constancy, spatial-relationships, position in space

Description: Place markers on the floor according to the ability level of students and the skills you wish to address. Divide the class into small groups of four to six students. Have the first students in line hop on each of the markers as they move to a designated spot and then reverse direction and hop back on the markers to return to their lines. The next student in each line will then perform the skill and the relay continues until all students have completed the task.

Variation: Add to the challenge by designating specific attributes of the markers on which students should hop. For example, have students find and hop only on triangle markers, or on red markers, or on small markers.

Hoop Relay

Equipment: hoops in different sizes

Task Analysis: muscular strength and endurance, cardiorespiratory endurance, bilateral activities, dynamic balance, body part awareness, eye-hand coordination, eye-hand accuracy, locomotor skills, explosive leg power, visual tracking skills, laterality skills, attention and concentration

Description: Divide the class into small groups of four to six students. Have the first students in line roll their hoops while moving forward to a designated spot and then return to their lines, handing off the hoops to the next students in line. The next students will then perform the skill and the relay continues until all students have completed the task.

Variation: Add to the challenge by selecting a locomotor movement for students to perform as they roll the hoops.

Partner Relay

Equipment: none

Task Analysis: muscular strength and endurance, cardiorespiratory endurance, bilateral activities, dynamic balance, body part awareness, locomotor skills, explosive leg power, socialization, cooperation, lateralization, crossing the midline, attention and concentration

Description: Divide the class into small groups of four to six students. Groups of even numbers of students work best in this relay. Choose a locomotor skill (e.g., marching). Have the first two students in each line hold hands, perform the locomotor skill to a designated spot, and then return to their line. The next pair of students in each line will then perform the skill and the relay continues until all students have completed the task.

Foot Dribbling Relay

Equipment: small balls in different sizes (decreasing the size of the balls increases the level of skill needed to complete the task)

Task Analysis: muscular strength and endurance, cardiorespiratory endurance, bilateral activities, dynamic balance, body part awareness, eye-foot coordination, eye-foot accuracy, locomotor skills, explosive leg power, visual tracking skills, crossing the midline, visual motor coordination, attention and concentration, figure-ground discrimination, form constancy, spatial relationships, position in space

Description: Divide the class into small groups of four to six students. Have the first students in line dribble balls with their feet—soccer style—while moving forward to a designated spot and then return to their lines, handing off the balls to the next students in line. The next students will then perform the skill and the relay continues until all students have completed the task.

Variation: Add to the challenge by selecting a locomotor movement for students to perform as they move.

Rope Jumping Relay

Equipment: jump ropes

Task Analysis: muscular strength and endurance, cardiorespiratory endurance, bilateral activities, dynamic balance, body part awareness, eye-foot coordination, eye-foot accuracy, locomotor skills, explosive leg power, visual tracking skills, eye-hand coordination, hypotonic, lateralization

Description: Divide the class into small groups of four to six students. Have the first students in line jump rope while moving forward to a designated spot and then return to their lines, handing off the jump ropes to the next students in line. The next students will then perform the skill and the relay continues until all students have completed the task.

Partner Toss and Catch Relay

Equipment: beanbags in different sizes

Task Analysis: muscular strength and endurance, cardiorespiratory endurance, bilateral activities, dynamic balance, body part awareness, eye-hand coordination, eye-hand accuracy, locomotor skills, explosive leg power, visual tracking skills, cooperation, socialization, crossing the midline, visual motor coordination, attention and concentration, figure-ground discrimination, form constancy, spatial relationships, position in space

Description: Divide the class into small groups of four to six students. Groups of even numbers of students work best in this relay. Have the first two students in each line toss and catch a beanbag as they move to a designated spot and then return to their line. The next pair of students in each line will then perform the skill and the relay continues until all students have completed the task.

Variation: Add to the challenge by selecting a locomotor movement for students to perform as they toss the beanbags back and forth.

Obstacle Course Relay

Equipment: a variety of obstacles found in the classroom

Task Analysis: motor planning and sequencing skills, muscular strength and endurance, cardiorespiratory endurance, bilateral activities, dynamic balance, body part awareness, eye-foot coordination, eye-foot accuracy, locomotor skills, explosive leg power, visual tracking skills, eye-hand coordination, directionality, crossing the midline, visual motor coordination, attention and concentration, figure-ground discrimination, form constancy, spatial relationships, position in space

Description: Use objects found in the classroom to design an obstacle course according to the ability level of students and the skills you wish to address. Use your imagination! For example, the challenge may be to hop through four hoops, crawl under two chairs, jump over a stack of four books, and bear walk around a wastebasket. Divide the class into small groups of four to six students. Have the first students in line complete the obstacle course and return to their lines. The next students in each line will then complete the course and the relay continues until all students have completed the task.

Scooter Board Relay

Equipment: scooter boards

Task Analysis: upper body muscular strength and endurance, cardiorespiratory endurance, bilateral activities, dynamic balance, body part awareness, laterality, upper body development, gross motor coordination, eye-foot accuracy, crossing the midline, visual motor coordination, attention and concentration, figure-ground discrimination, form constancy, spatial relationships, position in space, hypotonic

Description: Divide the class into small groups of four to six students. The first students in line should lie with their stomachs resting on the scooter boards and their legs extended. Have the students "walk" with their hands, moving forward to a designated spot and then returning to their lines, giving the scooter boards to the next students in line. The next students will then perform the skill and the relay continues until all students have completed the task.

Cross Over Relay

Equipment: straight lines on the floor

Task Analysis: crossing the midline, muscular strength and endurance, bilateral activities, dynamic balance, body part awareness, laterality, left/right concepts, gross motor coordination, visual motor integration, figure-ground discrimination, spatial relationships, position in space

Description: Divide the class into small groups of four to six students. Have the first student in each line walk along the line on the floor by crossing one foot over the line to the other side and then crossing back over the line with the other foot on the next step. Students move to a designated spot and then return to their lines. The next students in each line will then perform the skill and the relay continues until all students have completed the task.

Variations: I. Add to the challenge by selecting a locomotor movement or an animal walk for students to perform as they move.

2. Create wavy lines on the floor with masking tape for students to cross over as they move.

Carry the Bucket Relay

Equipment: plastic buckets, water

Task Analysis: motor planning, muscular strength and endurance, cardiorespiratory endurance, bilateral activities, dynamic balance, body part awareness, locomotor skills, hand strength, eye-hand coordination, spatial relationships, manipulative skills, finger dexterity, eye-hand accuracy

Description: This is a great outside activity for a hot day. Divide the class into small groups of four to six students. Place a bucket filled with water, with the water level marked, in front of each of the relay lines. Choose a locomotor movement (e.g., sliding) or an animal walk (e.g., bear walk). Have the first student in each line perform the movement to reach the bucket, pick it up, and bring the bucket back to the line. The next student in line will pick up the bucket, take it back to its original position, and perform the movement to return to the line. Have students continue until each has had a turn to carry the bucket. Look at the level of water remaining in each bucket, as the group who spilled the least amount of water wins.

Activity Cards Relay

Equipment: activity cards (found on pages 81–83)

Task Analysis: motor planning, muscular strength and endurance, cardiorespiratory endurance, bilateral activities, dynamic balance, body part awareness, locomotor skills, visual memory, cognition, language arts, crossing the midline, visual motor coordination, attention and concentration, figure-ground discrimination, form constancy, spatial relationships, position in space

Description: Divide the class into small groups of four to six students. Place each set of activity cards on the floor in front of the relay lines. Choose a locomotor movement (e.g., leaping) or an animal walk (e.g., horse gallop). Have the first student in each line perform the movement to reach the cards, read and do the activity that is on the first card, and perform the movement to return to the line. The next student in line will then perform the movement to reach the second card, read and do the activity, and perform the movement to return to the line. Have students continue until all of the activities have been performed. If you repeat the relay, make sure to mix up the order of the cards or change the order of the students so that they will face different challenges.

(activity cards)

Do 3 jumping jacks.

Turn around 3 times.

Touch your toes 6 times.

Clap your hands 4 times.

Stamp your feet 5 times.

Stand on your tiptoes and touch your head.

Jump on one foot 3 times.

Tap your knees 4 times.

Do 4 sit-ups.

Stretch as tall as you can 6 times.

Bend and touch your ankles 7 times.

Gallop in a circle.

Crawl in a straight line.

Walk 2 steps backward.

Touch your head and hop 5 times.

Take 2 giant leaps.

Take 4 giant steps forward.

Do 5 deep knee bends.

Fine Motor Relay Games

Eyedropper Relay

Equipment: eyedroppers, water, small cups

Task Analysis: motor planning, muscular strength and endurance, cardiorespiratory endurance, bilateral activities, dynamic balance, body part awareness, locomotor skills, visual memory, eye-hand coordination, spatial relationships, manipulative skills, visual discrimination, hand strength, finger dexterity, crossing the midline, visual motor coordination, attention and concentration, figure-ground discrimination, form constancy, position in space

Description: Divide the class into small groups of four to six students. Place an eyedropper, one small cup filled with water, and one small empty cup on the floor in front each of the relay lines. Choose a locomotor movement (e.g., walking) or an animal walk (e.g., bunny hop). Have the first student in each line perform the movement to reach the eyedropper and cups, use a tripod grip to fill the eyedropper with water from the first cup, squeeze the water into the second empty cup, and perform the movement to return to the line. The next student in line will then perform the movement, fill the eyedropper and squeeze the water into the second cup, and perform the movement to return to the line. Have students continue until all of the water has been transferred from the first cup to the second.

Nuts and Bolts Relay

Equipment: sets of nuts and bolts in different sizes

Task Analysis: motor planning, muscular strength and endurance, cardiorespiratory endurance, bilateral activities, dynamic balance, body part awareness, locomotor skills, visual memory, eye-hand coordination, spatial relationships, manipulative skills, visual discrimination, finger dexterity, eye-hand accuracy, form discrimination, cognition, crossing the midline, visual motor coordination, attention and concentration, figure-ground discrimination, form constancy, position in space

Description: Divide the class into small groups of four to six students. Place sets of nuts and bolts in different sizes in front of each of the relay lines. Choose a locomotor movement (e.g., hopping) or an animal walk (e.g., duck waddle). Have the first student in each line perform the movement to reach the nuts and bolts, find a nut and bolt set and screw the nut onto a bolt, and perform the movement to return to the line. The next student in line will perform the movement to reach the nuts and bolts, find a set to put together, and perform the movement to return to the line. Have students continue until all of the nuts and bolts have been matched correctly.

Cutting Relay

Equipment: enlarge dot to dot pictures on sturdy paper (dot to dot/lacing cards found on pages 86–90), safety scissors

Task Analysis: motor planning, muscular strength and endurance, cardiorespiratory endurance, bilateral activities, dynamic balance, body part awareness, locomotor skills, visual memory, cognition, shape formation, eye-hand coordination, eye-hand accuracy, spatial relationships, number or letter recognition, sequencing, visual motor integration

Description: Divide the class into small groups of four to six students. Place an enlarged dot to dot picture on the floor in front of each relay line. Place the safety scissors next to the picture. Choose a locomotor movement (e.g., tiptoeing) or an animal walk (e.g., leap frog). Have the first student in each line perform the movement to reach the picture, find the first number or letter and use the scissors to cut out the picture from the first dot to the second dot, and perform the movement to return to the line. The next student in line will perform the movement, cut from the second dot to the third dot, and perform the movement to return to the line. Have students continue cutting from dot to dot until the picture has been cut out.

Colorful Macaroni Relay

Equipment: colorful macaroni, small containers, yarn, colorful patterns of macaroni drawn on paper

Task Analysis: motor planning, muscular strength and endurance, cardiorespiratory endurance, bilateral activities, dynamic balance, body part awareness, locomotor skills, visual memory, eye-hand coordination, spatial relationships, manipulative skills, visual discrimination, finger dexterity, eye-hand accuracy, form discrimination, color recognition, sequencing, crossing the midline, visual motor coordination, attention and concentration, figure-ground discrimination, form constancy, position in space

Description: Divide the class into small groups of four to six students. Draw colorful patterns of macaroni on paper for each group. Place each group's pattern on the floor with a small container of colorful macaroni and a piece of yarn. Choose a locomotor movement (e.g., sliding) or an animal walk (e.g., monkey walk). Have the first student in each line perform the movement to reach the container of macaroni, look at the pattern, choose the first color of macaroni and string it on the yarn, and perform the movement to return to the line. The next student in line will then perform the movement, identify the next color of macaroni in the pattern, string it on the yarn, and perform the movement to return to the line. Have students continue to string the macaroni until the pattern is complete.

Lacing Relay

Equipment: enlarged dot to dot/lacing cards (found on page 86–90) on cardboard with holes punched on the dots, laces or pieces of yarn

Task Analysis: motor planning, muscular strength and endurance, cardiorespiratory endurance, bilateral activities, dynamic balance, body part awareness, locomotor skills, visual memory, cognition, shape formation, eye-hand coordination, eye-hand accuracy, spatial relationships, number recognition, sequencing, manipulative skills

Description: Divide the class into small groups of four to six students. Place an enlarged dot to dot picture and the lace on the floor in front of each relay line. Choose a locomotor movement (e.g., marching) or an animal walk (e.g., duck). Have the first student in each line perform the movement to reach the picture, find the first number or letter and use the lace to connect the first and second dots, and perform the movement to return to the line. The next student in line will then perform the movement, connect the second and third dots, and perform the movement to return to the line. Have students continue lacing to connect dot to dot in order until the picture is complete.

Variation: Provide sturdy paper or tagboard with dots indicated around the edges, a hole punch, and a lace for each relay line. Students may punch holes in the paper for the first part of the relay. When the punches are complete, they may continue the activity with a lacing relay.

Flamingo Dot to Dot

◆▼●■★◆▼●■★◆▼●■★◆▼●■★◆▼●■★◆▼●■★◆▼●■★◆▼●■★◆▼●■★◆▼●■★◆▼●■★◆▼

Snake Dot to Dot

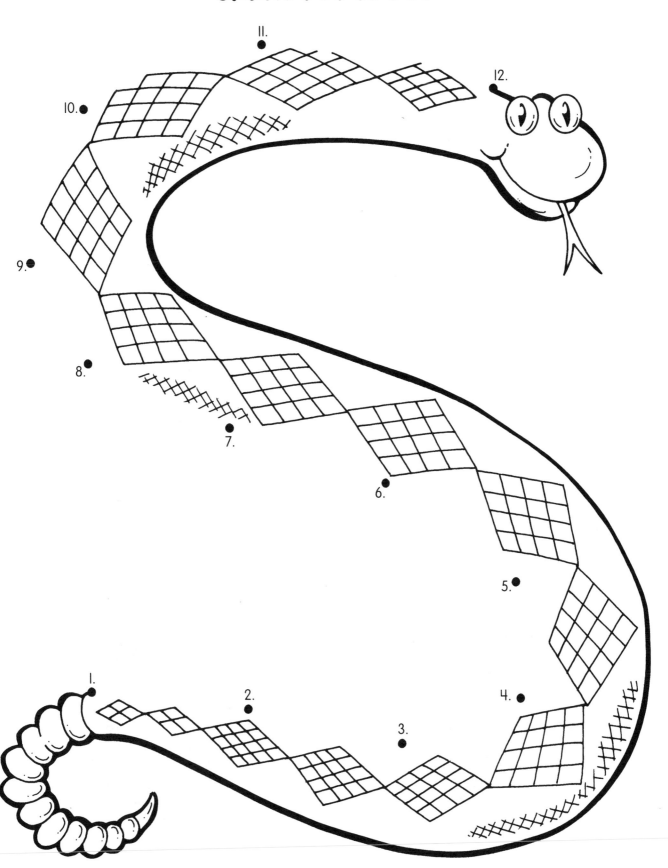

Car Dot to Dot

Pig Dot to Dot

Rabbit Dot to Dot

Early Learning Relay Games

Colorful Beanbag Toss Relay

Equipment: colorful beanbags, colorful hoops

Task Analysis: left/right concepts, motor planning, muscular strength and endurance, cardiorespiratory endurance, bilateral activities, dynamic balance, body part awareness, locomotor skills, visual memory, eye-hand coordination, eye-hand accuracy, spatial relationships, manipulative skills, visual tracking, laterality, crossing the midline, visual motor coordination, attention and concentration, figure-ground discrimination, form constancy, position in space, color recognition, color discrimination

Description: Divide the class into small groups of four to six students. Scatter a set of colorful hoops on the floor in front of each of the relay lines. Place a pile of colorful beanbags near each set of hoops. Choose a locomotor movement (e.g., galloping) or an animal walk (e.g., seal slide). Have the first student in each line perform the movement to reach the beanbags, use her right hand to select and toss a beanbag into the same color of hoop, and perform the movement to return to the line. The next student in line will perform the movement to reach the beanbags, use his right hand to choose and correctly toss a beanbag, and perform the movement to return to the line. Have students continue until all of the beanbags have been tossed into the correct color of hoop. Repeat the activity, having students use only their left hands to choose and toss the beanbags.

Body Part Identification Relay

Equipment: large outlines of a human body (drawn on paper for an inside relay or drawn outside with sidewalk chalk), crayons or sidewalk chalk, lists of body parts to identify

Task Analysis: left/right concepts, motor planning, muscular strength and endurance, cardiorespiratory endurance, bilateral activities, dynamic balance, body part awareness, locomotor skills, visual memory, eye-hand coordination, eye-hand accuracy, spatial relationships, manipulative skills, visual tracking, laterality, crossing the midline, visual motor coordination, attention and concentration, figure-ground discrimination, form constancy, position in space, graphomotor skills

Description: Divide the class into small groups of four to six students. Place a large outline of a human body in front of each relay line. Place the crayons and a reference list of body-part words next to the outline. Choose a locomotor movement (e.g., hopping) or an animal walk (e.g., crab scuttle). Have the first student in each line perform the movement to reach the outline of the body, select a body part (e.g., arm), use the crayon to write the correct word on the body part, and perform the movement to return to the line. The next student in line will then perform the movement, label another body part, and perform the movement to return to the line. Have students continue labeling until all of the selected body parts are identified.

Movement Word Relay

Equipment: movement word cards (found on pages 92–93)

Task Analysis: motor planning, muscular strength and endurance, cardiorespiratory endurance, bilateral activities, dynamic balance, body part awareness, locomotor skills, visual tracking skills, visual memory, cognition, language arts, spelling, word recognition, crossing the midline, visual motor coordination, attention and concentration, figure-ground discrimination, form constancy, spatial relationships, position in space

Description: Divide the class into small groups of four to six students. Scatter each set of movement word cards on the floor in front of the relay lines. Direct students to read the words on the cards and perform those movements back to the lines. Have the first student in each line run to the movement cards, read the word that is on the first card, and perform that movement as she returns to the line. The next student in line will then run to the second card, read the movement word, and perform the movement to return to the line. Have students continue until all of the movements have been performed.

walk backward	**skip**
dash	**creep**
spin in a circle	**stomp your feet**
jiggle	**crawl**

nod

trot

race

hop

run

scurry

sway

zigzag

Self-Help Sock Hop Relay

Equipment: students' shoes

Task Analysis: motor planning, muscular strength and endurance, cardiorespiratory endurance, bilateral activities, dynamic balance, body part awareness, eye-hand coordination, eye-hand accuracy, locomotor skills, visual tracking skills, visual memory, form discrimination, letter recognition, visual motor coordination, visual motor integration, figure-ground discrimination, spatial constancy, position in space

Description: Divide the class into small groups of four to six students. Have the groups form lines that radiate out; students will face toward the middle. Place all of the students' shoes in a mixed up pile in the center of the relay lines. Choose a locomotor movement (e.g., crawling) or an animal walk (e.g., turtle crawl). Have the first student in each line perform the movement to reach the pile of shoes, search to find one of her own shoes, put it on, and perform the movement to return to the line. Continue, with each student finding one shoe at a time, until all students have returned to their lines wearing both of their shoes.

Picture Matching Relay

Equipment: matching sets of pictures (picture cards found on pages 29–31), grids, beanbags

Task Analysis: motor planning, muscular strength and endurance, cardiorespiratory endurance, bilateral activities, dynamic balance, body part awareness, locomotor skills, visual memory, eye-hand coordination, eye-hand accuracy, spatial relationships, manipulative skills, visual discrimination, crossing the midline, visual motor coordination, attention and concentration, figure-ground discrimination, form constancy, position in space

Description: Divide the class into small groups of four to six students. Place a grid on the floor in front of each of the relay lines along with a pile of beanbags. Position a picture card in each square of the grid and then place the matching set of cards in a pile at the beginning of the relay lines. Choose a locomotor movement (e.g., jumping) or an animal walk (e.g., chicken walk). Have the first student in each line select a picture card, perform the movement to reach the beanbags, toss a beanbag into the square on the grid with the same picture, and perform the movement to return to the line. The next student in line will then choose a picture, perform the movement to reach the beanbags, toss a beanbag into the correct square, and perform the movement to return to the line. Have students continue until all of the picture cards have been matched correctly.

What's Missing? Relay

Equipment: "What's Missing?" cards (cards found on pages 95–96), crayons, construction paper

Task Analysis: motor planning, muscular strength and endurance, cardiorespiratory endurance, bilateral activities, dynamic balance, body part awareness, locomotor skills, visual memory, cognition, closure, visual discrimination, shape formation, crossing the midline, visual motor coordination, attention and concentration, figure-ground discrimination, form constancy, spatial relationships, position in space

Description: Divide the class into small groups of four to six students. Place each set of partially completed shape cards, the crayons, and the construction paper on the floor in front of the relay lines. Choose a locomotor movement (e.g., skipping) or an animal walk (e.g., turkey strut). Have the first student in each line perform the movement to reach the cards, choose a "What's Missing?" card, use a crayon on construction paper to redraw and complete the shape, and perform the movement to return to the line. The next student in line will perform the movement to reach the second "What's Missing?" card, draw on construction paper to complete the shape, and perform the movement to return to the line. Have students continue until each student has had a turn to complete a shape.

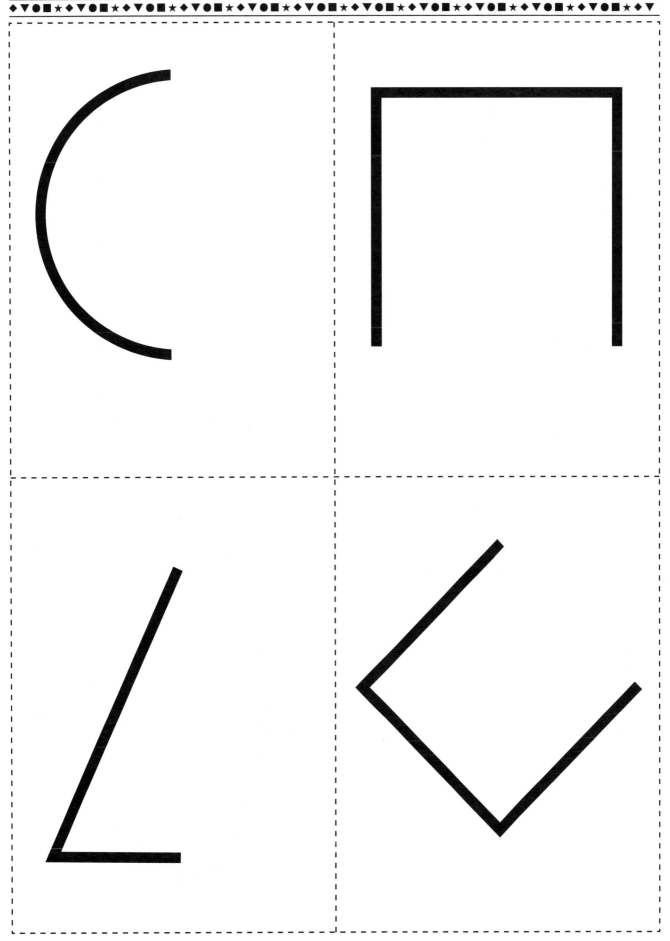

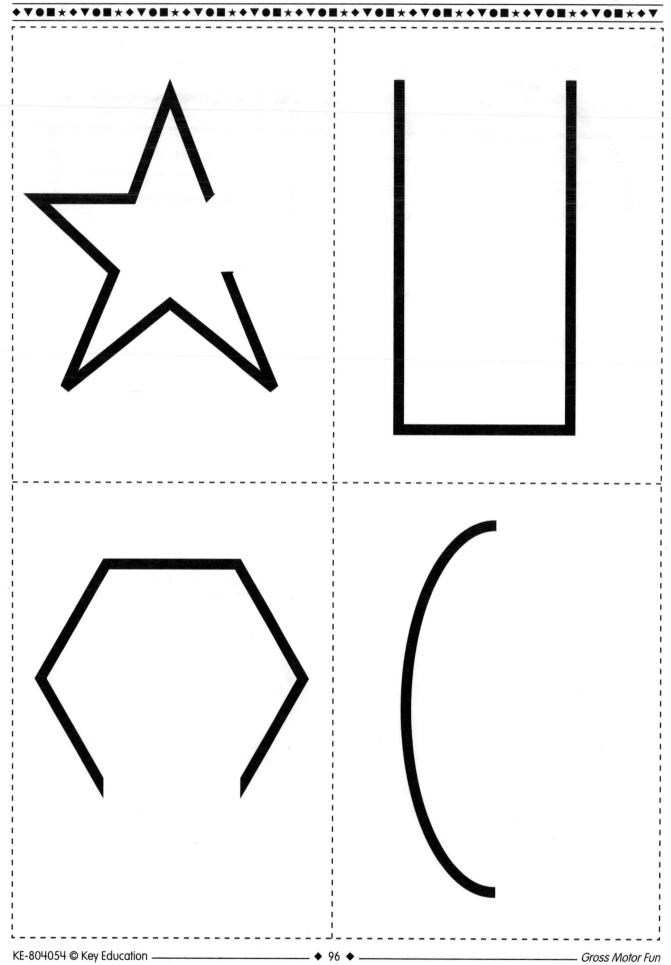

Puzzle Relay

Equipment: puzzles

Task Analysis: motor planning, muscular strength and endurance, cardiorespiratory endurance, bilateral activities, dynamic balance, body part awareness, eye-hand coordination, eye-hand accuracy, locomotor skills, visual tracking skills, visual memory, form discrimination, color recognition, graphomotor skills, spatial relationships, visual motor integration, figure-ground discrimination, form constancy, position in space, attention and concentration

Description: Divide the class into small groups of four to six students. Select the type of puzzle that is developmentally appropriate for your students. For each group, place a puzzle backboard or tray and the puzzle's pieces next to the backboard on the floor. Place a picture of the completed puzzle next to the pieces for reference. Choose a locomotor movement (e.g., walking) or an animal walk (e.g., seal slide). Have the first student in each line perform the movement to reach the puzzle, select a puzzle piece and place it on the backboard, and perform the movement to return to the line. The next student in line will then perform the movement, choose and add another piece to the puzzle, and perform the movement to return to the line. Have the relay continue until all of the puzzles are complete.

Matching Funny Faces Relay

Equipment: two copies of the reproducible funny faces (found on page 98), safety scissors, glue

Task Analysis: motor planning, muscular strength and endurance, cardiorespiratory endurance, bilateral activities, dynamic balance, body part awareness, locomotor skills, visual memory, eye-hand coordination, spatial relationships, manipulative skills, visual discrimination, finger dexterity, eye-hand accuracy, form discrimination, cognition, figure-ground discrimination, form constancy, position in space

Description: Divide the class into small groups of four to six students. Place a page of funny faces and scissors in front of each of the relay lines. Choose a locomotor movement (e.g., jumping) or an animal walk (e.g., elephant walk). Have the first student in each line perform the movement to reach the paper, use the scissors to cut out one funny face, and perform the movement to return to the line. The next student in line will then perform the movement to reach the paper, cut out a funny face, and perform the movement to return to the line. Have students continue until all of the faces are cut out. Then, place the glue and another page of funny faces next to the card faces in front of each of the relay lines. Have the first student in each line perform the movement to reach the funny faces card, choose a card face and glue it next to the matching face on the paper, and perform the movement to return to the line. The next student in line will then perform the movement to reach the card, glue a funny face next to its match, and perform the movement to return to the line. Have students continue until all of the faces have been matched correctly.

Funny Faces

Directions are found on page 97.

Language Arts Relay Games

Letter Search Relay

Equipment: opaque bags, large plastic letters, individual letter cards (found on pages 33–41)

Task Analysis: motor planning, muscular strength and endurance, cardiorespiratory endurance, bilateral activities, dynamic balance, body part awareness, eye-hand coordination, eye-hand accuracy, locomotor skills, visual tracking skills, visual memory, form discrimination, sequencing, cognition, crossing the midline, visual motor coordination, attention and concentration, figure-ground discrimination, form constancy, spatial relationships, position in space

Description: Divide the class into small groups of four to six students. Place the large plastic letters in the plastic bags and the letter cards on the floor in front of each relay line. Choose a locomotor movement (e.g., hopping) or an animal walk (e.g., elephant walk). Have the first student in each line perform the movement to reach the letter cards, select a letter, and then reach into the bag to feel, without looking, to find the selected letter. If the student chooses the correct plastic letter, she places it on the letter card and performs the movement to return to the line. If a student removes a letter from the bag that does not match the selected letter card, she replaces the letter in the bag and performs the movement back to the line. Continue the relay until all of the letter cards and plastic letters have been matched.

Building Letters Relay

Equipment: wooden cards in straight and curved pieces, individual letter cards (found on pages 33–41)

Task Analysis: motor planning, muscular strength and endurance, cardiorespiratory endurance, bilateral activities, dynamic balance, body part awareness, eye-hand coordination, eye-hand accuracy, locomotor skills, visual tracking skills, visual memory, form discrimination, letter recognition, visual motor coordination, visual motor integration, figure-ground discrimination, spatial constancy, position in space

Description: Divide the class into small groups of four to six students. Place the wooden cards and the letter cards on the floor in front of each relay line. Choose a locomotor movement (e.g., jumping) or an animal walk (e.g., bear walk). Have the first student in each line perform the movement to reach the letter cards, select a letter, choose a wooden card to begin forming the letter, and perform the movement to return to the line. The next student in line will then perform the movement, choose another wooden card, place it next to the first card to continue to make the letter, and perform the movement to return to the line. If at any time a student believes a card has been placed incorrectly, the student may use his turn to correct another student's card placement. Continue until all of the letters have been placed correctly.

Clay Letters Relay

Equipment: spelling words written on cards, clay

Task Analysis: motor planning, muscular strength and endurance, cardiorespiratory endurance, bilateral activities, dynamic balance, body part awareness, locomotor skills, visual memory, eye-hand coordination, spatial relationships, manipulative skills, visual discrimination, hand strength, finger dexterity, crossing the midline, visual motor coordination, attention and concentration, figure-ground discrimination, form constancy, position in space

Description: Divide the class into small groups of four to six students. Place a spelling word card and a lump of clay in front of each relay line. Choose a locomotor movement (e.g., marching) or an animal walk (e.g., horse gallop). Have the first student in each line perform the movement to reach the word card, read the word, form the first letter of the word out of the clay, place it on the floor, and perform the movement to return to the line. The next student in line will then perform the movement, read the word and form the second letter, place it next to the first letter, and perform the movement to return to the line. If a student believes the letters are not in order, the student may use her turn to correct the spelling. Have students continue forming letters until each word is spelled correctly and legibly.

Letter Recognition Relay

Equipment: large cards of capital letters, pictures cut from magazines, glue

Task Analysis: motor planning, muscular strength and endurance, cardiorespiratory endurance, bilateral activities, dynamic balance, body part awareness, eye-hand coordination, eye-hand accuracy, locomotor skills, visual tracking skills, visual memory, form discrimination, sequencing, cognition, language arts, letter recognition

Description: Divide the class into small groups of four to six students. Place a large card of a capital letter, pictures cut from magazines, and glue on the floor in front of each of the relay lines. Choose a locomotor movement (e.g., walking) or an animal walk (e.g., spider scurry). Have the first student in each line perform the movement to reach the letter card, find a magazine picture of something that begins with that letter, glue the picture to the letter, and perform the movement to return to the line. The next student in line will then perform the movement to reach the letter, find another picture that begins with the letter, glue it to the letter card, and perform the movement to return to the line. Have students continue the relay until all of the students have chosen and glued a picture to the letter.

Fishing for Spelling Words Relay

Equipment: word cards, buckets of water, magnetic letters, fishing rods (made by attaching a string and magnet to a dowel)

Task Analysis: motor planning, muscular strength and endurance, cardiorespiratory endurance, bilateral activities, dynamic balance, body part awareness, eye-hand coordination, eye-hand accuracy, locomotor skills, visual tracking skills, visual memory, form discrimination, sequencing, cognition, language arts, letter recognition, spelling skills, crossing the midline, visual motor coordination, attention and concentration, figure-ground discrimination, form constancy, spatial relationships, position in space

Description: Divide the class into small groups of four to six students. Place a bucket of water with magnetic letters, spelling word cards, and a magnetic fishing pole on the floor in front of each relay line. Choose a locomotor movement (e.g., skipping) or an animal walk (e.g., kangaroo hop). Have the first student in each line perform the movement to reach the fishing pole, choose a word card, use the fishing pole to catch the first letter in the word and place it next to the word card, and perform the movement to return to the line. The next student in line will then perform the movement, use the fishing pole to catch the second letter in the chosen word, place it next to the first letter, and perform the movement to return to the line. If a student believes the letters have not been chosen or ordered correctly, the student may use his turn to correct the letters. Have students continue the relay until all of the words are spelled correctly.

Variation: Write spelling words on fish (pattern below). One student will catch a fish and then read the word. Another student must spell the word correctly.

(fish pattern)

◆▼●■★◆▼●■★◆▼●■★◆▼●■★◆▼●■★◆▼●■★◆▼●■★◆▼●■★◆▼●■★◆▼●■★◆▼

Letter Stamps Relay

Equipment: letter stamp kits, construction paper, vocabulary words written on cards

Task Analysis: motor planning, muscular strength and endurance, cardiorespiratory endurance, bilateral activities, dynamic balance, body part awareness, eye-hand coordination, eye-hand accuracy, locomotor skills, visual tracking skills, visual memory, form discrimination, graphomotor skills, sequencing, cognition, language arts, visual memory, figure-ground discrimination, spatial relationships, attention and concentration, sequencing, fine motor skills

Description: Divide the class into small groups of four to six students. Place the letter stamp kits, construction paper, and vocabulary word cards on the floor in front of each relay line. Choose a locomotor movement (e.g., bouncing) or an animal walk (e.g., elephant stomp). Have the first student in each line perform the movement to reach the vocabulary word card, read the word, and choose the stamp of the letter that begins the word. The student should stamp the first letter on the construction paper and perform the movement to return to the line. The next student in line will then perform the movement, choose and stamp the second letter of the vocabulary word, and perform the movement to return to the line. If at any time a student believes a letter has been stamped incorrectly, the student may use his turn to correct another student's answer. Each group continues until the vocabulary word has been spelled correctly.

Color by Word Relay

Equipment: pictures (reproducible color by word pictures found on pages 102–106); crayons broken into 1" (2.54 cm) pieces to facilitate the tripod grip

Task Analysis: motor planning, muscular strength and endurance, cardiorespiratory endurance, bilateral activities, dynamic balance, body part awareness, eye-hand coordination, eye-hand accuracy, locomotor skills, visual tracking skills, visual memory, form discrimination, color recognition, graphomotor skills, visual motor integration, spatial relationships, form constancy

Description: Divide the class into small groups of four to six students. For each group, place an enlarged picture to color on the wall or floor. Place the crayons next to the picture. Choose a locomotor movement (e.g., skipping) or an animal walk (e.g., duck waddle). Have the first student in each line perform the movement to reach the picture, choose a crayon and color in the correct space, and perform the movement to return to the line. The next student in line will then perform the movement, color in another space, and perform the movement to return to the line. Have students continue the relay until each picture is complete.

Toss and Spell Relay

Equipment: beanbags; individual letter cards (found on pages 33–41); vocabulary words written on cards

Task Analysis: motor planning, muscular strength and endurance, cardiorespiratory endurance, bilateral activities, dynamic balance, body part awareness, locomotor skills, visual tracking skills, visual memory, form discrimination, sequencing, cognition, crossing the midline, visual motor coordination, attention and concentration, figure-ground discrimination, form constancy, spatial relationships, position in space, visual motor integration, eye-hand accuracy, language arts

Description: Divide the class into small groups of four to six students. Scatter the individual letter cards and place the beanbags on the floor in front of each relay line. Choose a locomotor movement (e.g., skipping) or an animal walk (e.g., chicken walk). Review the vocabulary words. Then, select and hold up a vocabulary word for all of the teams to spell. Have the first student in each line perform the movement to reach the beanbags and individual letter cards, toss a beanbag on the letter that begins the vocabulary word, and perform the movement to return to the line. The next student in line will then perform the movement, toss a beanbag on the second letter of the vocabulary word, and perform the movement to return to the line. If at any time a student believes a beanbag has been tossed on a letter incorrectly, the student may use his turn to correct another student's answer. Continue the relay until the vocabulary word has been spelled correctly by all of the groups.

Color by Word: Kite

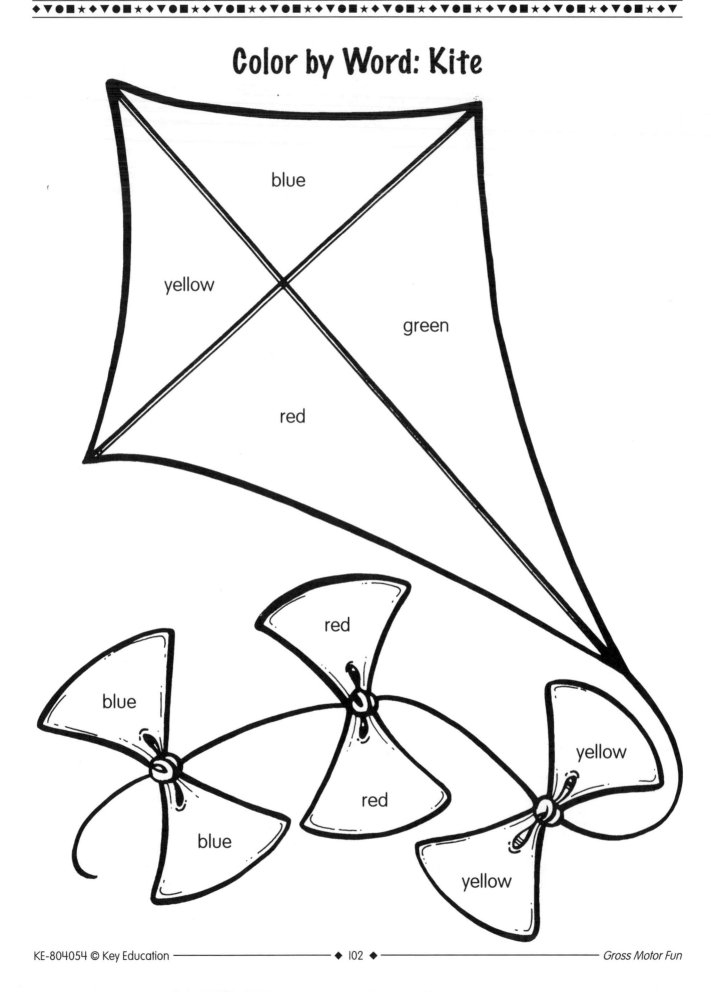

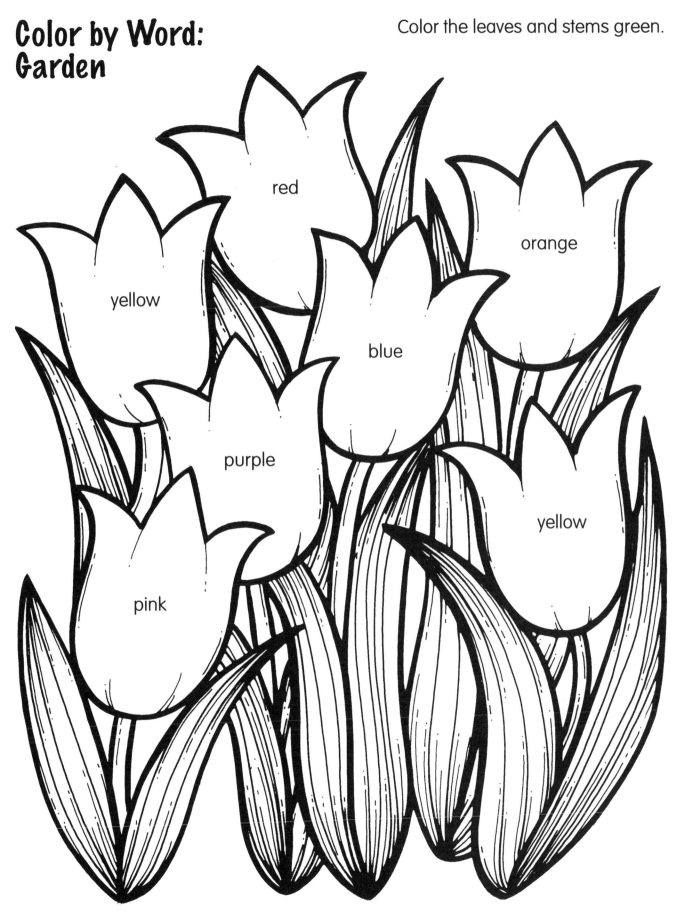

Color by Word: Garden

Color the leaves and stems green.

Color by Word: Balloons

Color the bow red.

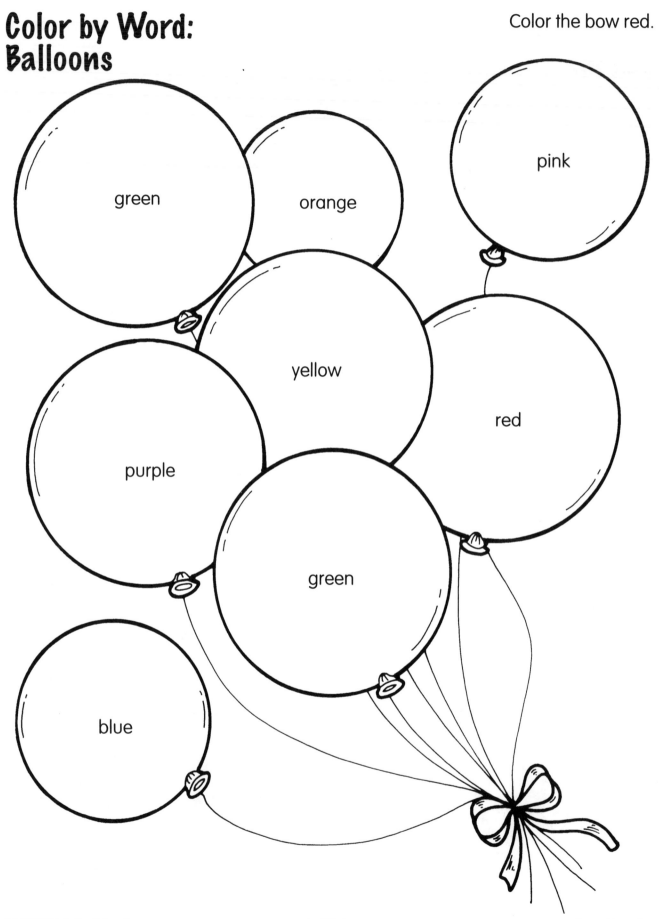

Color by Word: Toucan

Color the leaves green.
Color the branch brown.

Color by Word: Fish Aquarium

Color the rocks and sand brown.
Color the seaweed green.
Color the water blue.

Sponge Spelling Relay
Equipment: l" x l" (2.54 cm x 2.54 cm) sponges, washable paint, paint trays, spelling words (written on cards and laminated), construction paper

Task Analysis: motor planning, muscular strength and endurance, cardiorespiratory endurance, bilateral activities, dynamic balance, body part awareness, locomotor skills, visual memory, eye-hand coordination, spatial relationships, manipulative skills, visual discrimination, finger dexterity, eye-hand accuracy, form discrimination, cognition, sequencing letters, crossing the midline, visual motor coordination, attention and concentration, figure-ground discrimination, form constancy, position in space, graphomotor skills

Description: Divide the class into small groups of four to six students. Place a sponge, a small tray of paint, a piece of construction paper, and a spelling word card on the floor in front of each of the relay lines. Choose a locomotor movement (e.g., skipping) or an animal walk (e.g., inchworm inch). Have the first student in each line perform the movement to reach the sponge and paint, use a tripod grip to pick up the sponge, and load the sponge with paint. The student should then look at the spelling word, use the sponge to write its first letter on the construction paper, and perform the movement to return to the line. The next student in line will then perform the movement, use the sponge to write the second letter of the spelling word, and perform the movement to return to the line. Have students continue the relay until each groups' word is spelled correctly.

Spelling Relay
Equipment: white construction paper, crayons broken into l" (2.54 cm) pieces to facilitate the tripod grip, lists of chosen spelling words

Task Analysis: motor planning, muscular strength and endurance, cardiorespiratory endurance, bilateral activities, dynamic balance, body part awareness, eye-hand coordination, eye-hand accuracy, locomotor skills, visual tracking skills, visual memory, form discrimination, letter recognition, graphomotor skills, crossing the midline, visual motor coordination, attention and concentration, figure-ground discrimination, form constancy, spatial relationships, position in space

Description: Divide the class into small groups of four to six students. For each group, write the first letter of several spelling words on construction paper and draw blank lines for the remaining letters of each of the words. Place the crayons next to the construction paper. Display a list of the chosen spelling words near the construction paper for reference. Choose a locomotor movement (e.g., galloping) or an animal walk (e.g., elephant walk). Have the first student in each line perform the movement to reach the construction paper, use the crayon to write the second letter of the spelling word on the blank, and perform the movement to return to the line. The next student in line will then perform the movement, write the next letter, and perform the movement to return to the line. If a student believes a letter is written incorrectly, the student may use his turn to correct the spelling. Have students continue writing letters until the spelling words are complete. Repeat with new spelling words.

Read the Sentences Relay
Equipment: simple sentences containing action verbs, written on sentence strips

Task Analysis: motor planning, muscular strength and endurance, cardiorespiratory endurance, bilateral activities, dynamic balance, body part awareness, eye-hand coordination, eye-hand accuracy, locomotor skills, visual tracking skills, visual memory, form discrimination, cognition, language arts, spelling, crossing the midline, visual motor coordination, attention and concentration, figure-ground discrimination, form constancy, spatial relationships, position in space

Description: Divide the class into small groups of four to six students. Place the sentence strips on the floor in front of the relay lines. Choose a locomotor movement (e.g., tiptoeing) or an animal walk (e.g., frog leap). Have the first student in each line perform the movement to reach the sentence strips, choose the first sentence to read aloud (e.g., "The brown fox can run fast."), set it apart from the others, and then perform the action word in the sentence (e.g., run) to return to the line. The next student in line will then perform the movement, read the second sentence, and perform the action word to return to the line. Have students continue the relay until each student has read a sentence.

Sequence the Story Relay

Equipment: short story, narrative, or nursery rhyme (nursery rhyme picture cards found on pages 108–112)

Task Analysis: motor planning, muscular strength and endurance, cardiorespiratory endurance, bilateral activities, dynamic balance, body part awareness, eye-hand coordination, eye-hand accuracy, locomotor skills, visual tracking skills, visual memory, form discrimination, sequencing, cognition, language arts, visual memory, figure-ground discrimination, spatial relationships, attention and concentration

Description: Divide the class into small groups of four to six students. Read a short story, narrative, or nursery rhyme to students. Place the pictures of the events in the story or rhyme on the floor in front of each relay line. Choose a locomotor movement (e.g., galloping) or an animal walk (e.g., bear walk). Have the first student in each line perform the movement to reach the pictures, find the picture of the first event in the story, place it to the side, and perform the movement to return to the line. The next student in line will then perform the movement, find the picture of the second event, place it next to the first picture, and perform the movement to return to the line. If at any time a student believes a picture has been placed incorrectly, the student may use his turn to correct another student's answer. Continue the relay until each group's story picture sequence is complete.

(nursery rhyme sequencing cards)

Math Relay Games

What Is It? Relay

Equipment: enlarged dot to dot pictures (dot to dot/lacing cards found on pages 86–90), easel, crayons

Task Analysis: motor planning, muscular strength and endurance, cardiorespiratory endurance, bilateral activities, dynamic balance, body part awareness, locomotor skills, visual memory, cognition, language arts, closure, visual discrimination, form constancy, spatial relationships, position in space, visual motor coordination, crossing the midline, visual motor integration, attention and concentration, shape formation, graphomotor skills

Description: Divide the class into small groups of four to six students. For each group, place an enlarged dot to dot picture with its title covered on the wall or easel. Place the crayons next to the picture. Choose a locomotor movement (e.g., hopping) or an animal walk (e.g., inchworm inch). Have the first student in each line perform the movement to reach the picture, find the first number, and use a crayon to connect the first two dots. Then, the student may guess what the completed picture will be and perform the movement to return to the line. The next student in line will perform the movement, connect the second and third dots, make a guess about the picture, and perform the movement to return to the line. Have students continue connecting the dots until each picture has been identified or the dot to dots are complete.

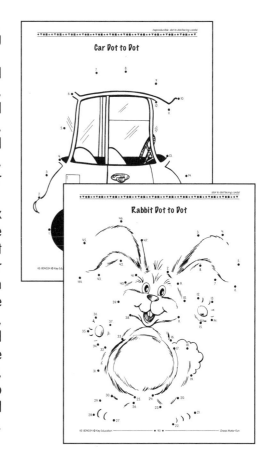

Let's Get Organized Relay

Equipment: gallon size resealable plastic bags, variety of school supplies (such as pencils, pens, markers, erasers, crayons, paper clips, rulers), school tools sequencing strips (found on pages 114–116)

Task Analysis: motor planning, muscular strength and endurance, cardiorespiratory endurance, bilateral activities, dynamic balance, body part awareness, eye-hand coordination, eye-hand accuracy, locomotor skills, visual tracking skills, visual memory, form discrimination, sequencing, cognition, language arts, visual memory, figure-ground discrimination, spatial relationships, attention and concentration, sequencing, fine motor skills

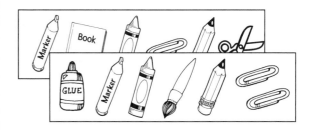

Description: Divide the class into small groups of four to six students. Place the resealable plastic bags, the school supplies, and the sequencing strips on the floor in front of each relay line. Choose a locomotor movement (e.g., striding) or an animal walk (e.g., spider scurry). Have the first student in each line perform the movement to reach the card, identify the first school supply on the strip, find the matching item, and open the resealable bag and place the item in it. Then, the student should close the bag (using a fine motor tripod grip) and perform the movement to return to the line. The next student in line will then perform the movement, identify and find the second item, open the bag, and place the item inside. After closing the bag, the student performs the movement to return to the line. If at any time a student believes an item has been placed in the bag incorrectly, the student may use his turn to correct the error. Continue the relay until all of the school supplies are organized in the bag.

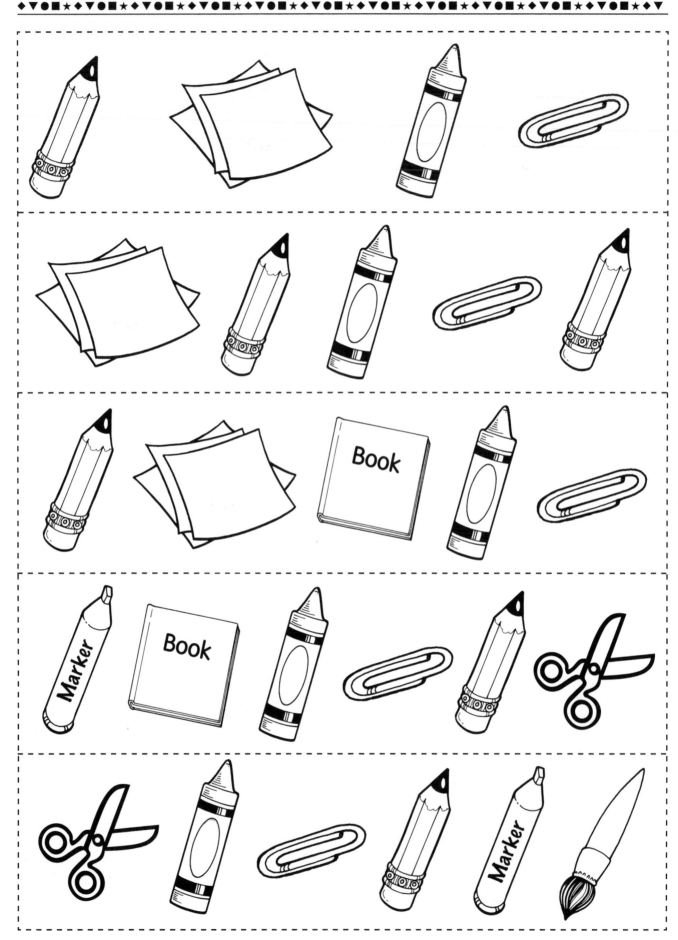

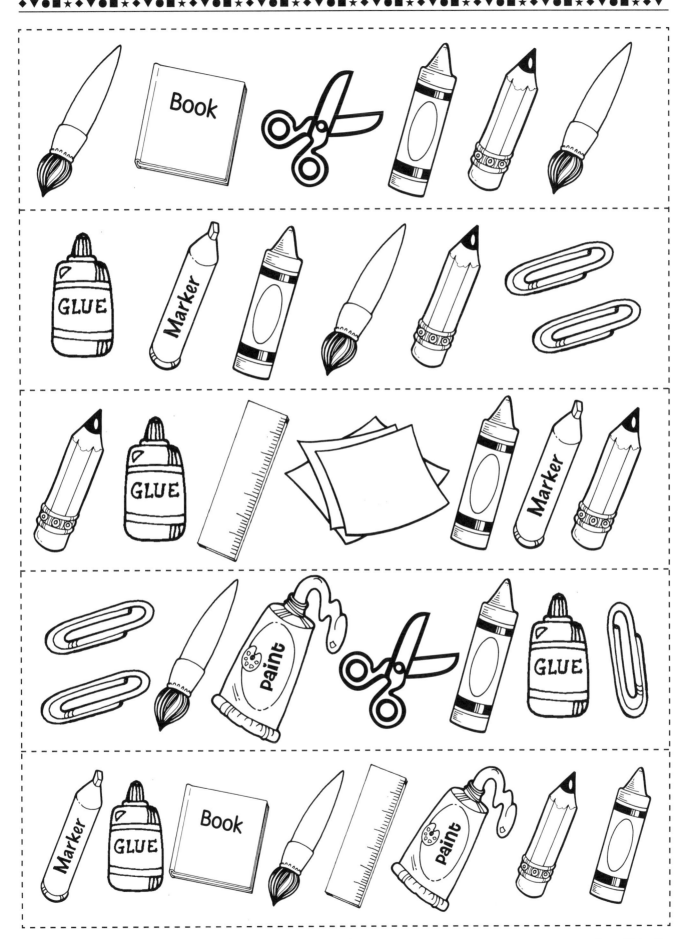

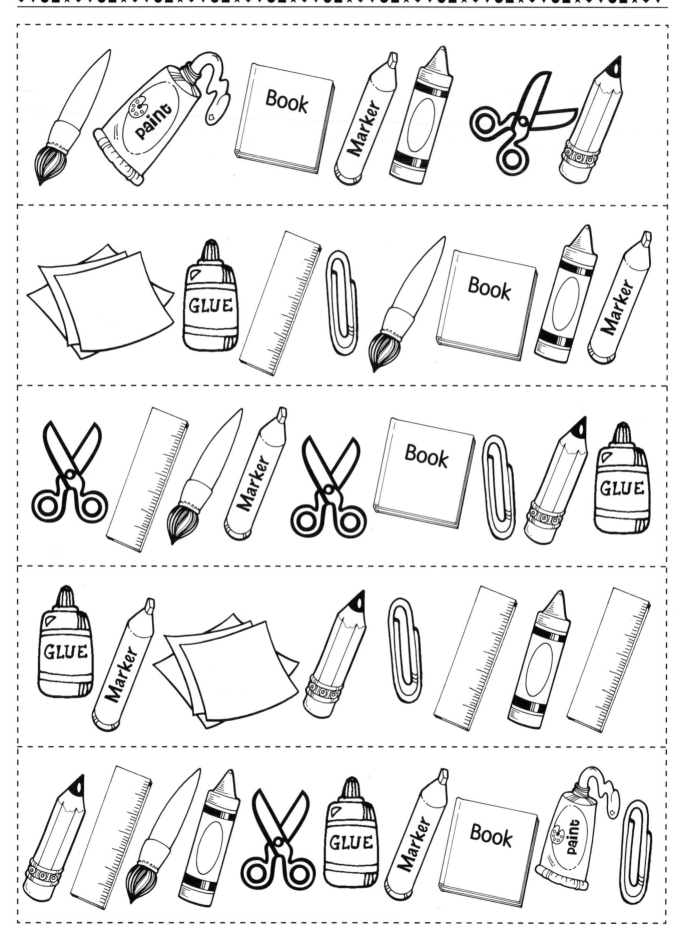

◆▼●■★◆▼●■★◆▼●■★◆▼●■★◆▼●■★◆▼●■★◆▼●■★◆▼●■★◆▼●■★◆▼●■★◆▼●■★◆▼

Colorful Clothespin Pattern Relay

Equipment: colorful clothespins, shoe boxes, color patterns on cards

Task Analysis: motor planning, muscular strength and endurance, cardiorespiratory endurance, bilateral activities, dynamic balance, body part awareness, locomotor skills, visual memory, cognition, shape formation, eye-hand coordination, eye-hand accuracy, spatial relationships, number recognition, sequencing, manipulative skills, crossing the midline, visual motor coordination, attention and concentration, figure-ground discrimination, form constancy, position in space

Description: Divide the class into small groups of four to six students. Place a shoe box, colorful clothespins, and a color pattern on the floor in front of each of the relay lines. Choose a locomotor movement (e.g., sliding) or an animal walk (e.g., monkey walk). Have the first student in each line perform the movement to reach the pattern and shoe box, choose the clothespin that is the first color in the pattern and place it on the edge of the shoe box, and perform the movement to return to the line. The next student in line will then perform the movement, choose the color of clothespin that is the second in the pattern, place it next to the first clothespin on the box, and perform the movement to return to the line. If a student believes the clothespins are not in order, the student may use her turn to correct the order. Have students continue the relay until the patterns are complete.

Smallest to Largest (or Shortest to Tallest) Relay

Equipment: any objects that can be sequentially sized from smallest to largest (e.g., six wooden pegs ranging from 1" to 6" [2.54 cm to 15.24 cm] in diameter)

Task Analysis: motor planning, muscular strength and endurance, cardiorespiratory endurance, bilateral activities, dynamic balance, body part awareness, eye-hand coordination, eye-hand accuracy, locomotor skills, visual tracking skills, visual memory, form discrimination, sequencing, cognition, fine motor skills, finger dexterity, visual motor integration, figure-ground discrimination, form constancy, spatial relationships, position in space

Description: Divide the class into small groups of four to six students. Scatter each set of objects on the floor in front of the relay lines. Direct students to place the objects on the floor in order from smallest to largest. Choose a locomotor movement (e.g., hopping) or an animal walk (e.g., crab scuttle). Have the first student in each line perform the movement to reach the objects, choose the smallest object, set it apart from the others, and perform the movement to return to the line. The next student in line will then perform the movement, choose the object that is next smallest, place it next to the smallest object, and perform the movement to return to the line. If a student believes the objects are not in order, the student may use his turn to correct the order of the objects. Have students continue the relay until all of the objects are placed from smallest to largest.

Cut Out the Fraction Relay

Equipment: fraction flash cards (found on pages 118–120), pieces of paper with lines dividing them into equal segments (halves, thirds, fourths, fifths, sixths), safety scissors, crayons

Task Analysis: motor planning, muscular strength and endurance, cardiorespiratory endurance, bilateral activities, dynamic balance, body part awareness, eye-hand coordination, eye-hand accuracy, locomotor skills, visual tracking skills, visual memory, form discrimination, sequencing, cognition, math skills, number counting, position in space, form constancy, graphomotor skills

Description: Divide the class into small groups of four to six students. Place fraction flash cards, paper divided into segments, safety scissors, and crayons in front of each of the relay lines. Choose a locomotor movement (e.g., leaping) or an animal walk (e.g., bunny hop). Have the first student in each line perform the movement to reach the fraction flash cards and select a card. Then, the student should find a piece of segmented paper divided into the matching number of pieces, use the scissors to cut out the same fractional piece that is written on the flash card, write the fraction on the piece with the crayon, and perform the movement to return to the line. If at any time a student believes a fraction has been incorrectly represented, the student may use his turn to correct another student's fraction. Continue the relay until each student has chosen a fraction flash card and cut out and labeled the matching fractional piece.

1/2

1/3

1/4

1/5

2/3

3/4

2/5

3/5

1/6

2/6

4/6

5/6

Playing Cards Relay

Equipment: deck of playing cards (aces through 10s with no face cards), number sentence flash cards with a missing addend or sum (found on pages 122–126)

Task Analysis: motor planning, muscular strength and endurance, cardiorespiratory endurance, bilateral activities, dynamic balance, body part awareness, eye-hand coordination, eye-hand accuracy, locomotor skills, visual tracking skills, visual memory, form discrimination, sequencing, cognition, math skills, number counting, position in space, form constancy

Description: Divide the class into small groups of four to six students. Place the playing cards and flash cards in front of each of the relay lines. Choose a locomotor movement (e.g., sliding) or an animal walk (e.g., snake slither). Have the first student in each line perform the movement to reach the flash cards and select a card. The student should then find a playing card to complete the number sentence on the flash card, place both cards on the floor, and perform the movement to return to the line. If at any time a student believes a number sentence has not been completed correctly, the student may use her turn to correct another student's number sentence. Continue the relay until each student has completed a number sentence.

Dominoes Relay

Equipment: sets of dominoes

Task Analysis: motor planning, muscular strength and endurance, cardiorespiratory endurance, bilateral activities, dynamic balance, body part awareness, eye-hand coordination, eye-hand accuracy, locomotor skills, visual tracking skills, visual memory, form discrimination, sequencing, cognition, position in space, form constancy, spatial relationships, counting and number recognition

Description: Divide the class into small groups of four to six students. Place the dominoes on the floor in front of each relay line. Choose a locomotor movement (e.g., galloping) or an animal walk (e.g., bear walk). Have the first student in each line perform the movement to reach the dominoes, select a domino, place it apart from the pile of dominoes, and perform the movement to return to the line. The next student in line will then perform the movement, find a domino to match the first domino, place it correctly next to the first, and perform the movement to return to the line. If at any time a student believes a domino has been placed incorrectly, the student may use his turn to correct another student's answer. Continue the relay until all of the possible domino matches have been made.

Sorting Geometric Shapes Relay

Equipment: a variety of geometric shapes, geometric shape picture cards

Task Analysis: motor planning, muscular strength and endurance, cardiorespiratory endurance, bilateral activities, dynamic balance, body part awareness, eye-hand coordination, eye-hand accuracy, locomotor skills, visual tracking skills, visual memory, form discrimination, letter recognition, visual motor coordination, visual motor integration, figure-ground discrimination, spatial constancy, position in space

Description: Divide the class into small groups of four to six students. Place the geometric shapes and the geometric shape picture cards on the floor in front of each relay line. Choose a locomotor movement (e.g., skipping) or an animal walk (e.g., kangaroo hop). Have the first student in each line perform the movement to reach the picture cards, select a card, find the matching geometric shape and place it on the picture card, and perform the movement to return to the line. If at any time a student believes a geometric shape has been placed incorrectly, the student may use her turn to correct another student's placement. Continue the relay until each student has sorted a geometric shape.

Cutting Straws Math Relay

Equipment: number sentence flash cards with no sums (found on pages 124–126), plastic straws, safety scissors

Task Analysis: motor planning, muscular strength and endurance, cardiorespiratory endurance, bilateral activities, dynamic balance, body part awareness, eye-hand coordination, eye-hand accuracy, locomotor skills, visual tracking skills, visual memory, form discrimination, sequencing, cognition, position in space, form constancy, spatial relationships, math skills

Description: Divide the class into small groups of four to six students. Place the flash cards with number sentences, scissors, and plastic straws on the floor in front of each relay line. Choose a locomotor movement (e.g., leaping) or an animal walk (e.g., inchworm inch). Have the first student in each line perform the movement to reach the flash cards, read the first problem (e.g., $2 + 6 = \_\_$), and solve it. Then, the student will use the scissors to cut a straw into the same number of pieces as the answer to the flash card problem (e.g., 8) and place the pieces of straw on the flash card. The student should perform the movement to return to the line. Have students continue the relay until each student has solved a problem and recorded the answer with pieces of a straw. Allow the group of students who finishes the relay first to read the problems and count the straw pieces for the class.

Fill in the Blank Number Sentences Relay

Equipment: sets of number sentence problems (covering concepts you are currently working on in class) written on construction paper, crayons

Task Analysis: motor planning, muscular strength and endurance, cardiorespiratory endurance, bilateral activities, dynamic balance, body part awareness, eye-hand coordination, eye-hand accuracy, locomotor skills, visual tracking skills, visual memory, form discrimination, graphomotor skills, sequencing, cognition, math skills, crossing the midline, visual motor coordination, attention and concentration, figure-ground discrimination, form constancy, spatial relationships, position in space

Description: Divide the class into small groups of four to six students. Write number sentence problems on construction paper, one set of problems for each group. This game is a great way to review information that has been taught, to prepare for a quiz, or to pretest students' knowledge when presenting new material. Direct students to fill in the missing number that will make each number sentence correct. Place the problems on the floor or wall along with crayons. Choose a locomotor movement (e.g., sliding) or an animal walk (e.g., chicken walk). Have the first student in each line perform the movement to reach the page of problems, answer the first question by filling in the missing number, and perform the movement to return to the line. The next student in line will then perform the movement, fill in the answer for the next problem, and perform the movement to return to the line. Have students continue the relay until all of the problems have been answered. If a student believes a number written by a classmate is not correct, the student may use his turn to correct the problem. Then, review all of the answers and congratulate the group with the most correct answers.

(number sentence cards)

$$\square + 4 = 6$$

$$3 + \square = 5$$

$$4 + \square = 7$$

$$3 + \square = 6$$

$$\square + 4 = 8$$

$$\square + 5 = 9$$

$1 + 2 =$ ☐

$2 + 2 =$ ☐

$3 + 1 =$ ☐

$3 + 2 =$ ☐

$3 + 3 =$ ☐

$4 + 2 =$ ☐

4 + 1 =

2 + 5 =

3 + 4 =

1 + 6 =

2 + 6 =

3 + 5 =

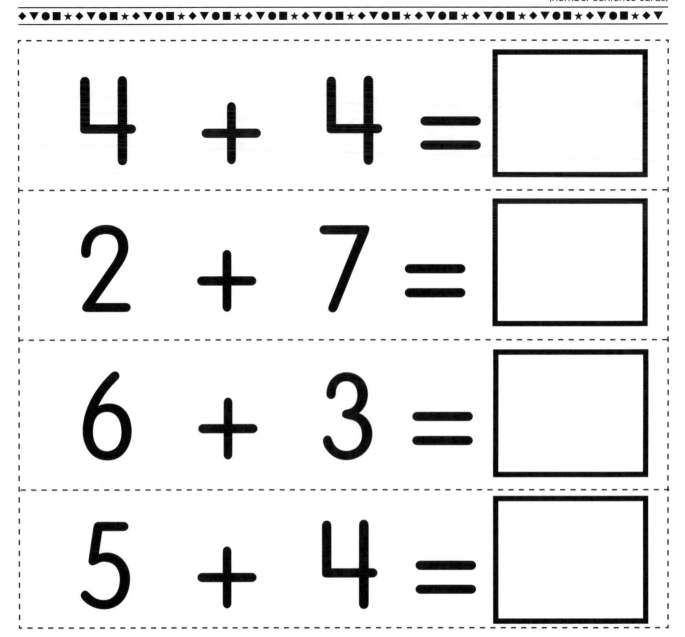

Let's Roll the Dice Number Sentence Relay

Equipment: pairs of dice, crayons, construction paper

Task Analysis: motor planning, muscular strength and endurance, cardiorespiratory endurance, bilateral activities, dynamic balance, body part awareness, eye-hand coordination, eye-hand accuracy, locomotor skills, visual tracking skills, visual memory, form discrimination, graphomotor skills, sequencing, cognition, language arts, visual memory, figure-ground discrimination, spatial relationships, attention and concentration, sequencing, fine motor skills

Description: Divide the class into small groups of four to six students. Place the dice, crayons, and construction paper on the floor in front of each relay line. Choose a locomotor movement (e.g., jumping) or an animal walk (e.g., bear walk). Have the first student in each line perform the movement to reach the dice, roll them to select the addends for a number sentence, write the addition problem on the construction paper, and solve it. Then, the student should place the dice next to the addends on the written equation and perform the movement to return to the line. If at any time a student believes a number sentence has been written incorrectly, the student may use his turn to correct another student's answer. Continue the relay until all students have rolled the dice to create and solve number sentences.

Variation: Students may use the pair of numbers rolled to create subtraction, multiplication, and division number sentences.

Chapter 4: Creative Rhythms and Movement

A changing society and lifestyles based on high technology contribute to the fact that many children are not experiencing the natural movement necessary for normal development. Today, opportunities for movement are often not spontaneous, such as playing in the neighborhood after school, but rather require structure and to be scheduled as events. As a result, children, especially those with special needs, can benefit from intentional opportunities to explore creative body movements through nonthreatening and experiential activities.

Active, natural play and movements assist and regulate the developing central nervous system. Engaging in natural activities stimulates the tactile, visual, auditory, proprioceptive, and vestibular systems. This strengthens perceptual-motor development. Use the creative rhythm and movement activities in this chapter to offer overall support for this developing motor domain.

Objectives of the Movement Program

For the Teacher:

- To develop an awareness of movement or "kinesthetic sympathy" for each child; Kinesthetic sympathy means an understanding and responsiveness by the teacher to that which is involved in a specific movement. To do this, one needs to practice the ability to observe children, for example, watching a child run and knowing the effort, quality, and feeling the child gives to the action.

For the Students:

- To create a joy in movement

- To develop a natural flow, rhythm, and flexible use of the body in basic movements so that children can explore their environment freely and with assurance

- To assist children in developing an awareness of their bodies and how they function; to integrate this knowledge so that it may be used in an organized way, bringing confidence when attempting new activities

- To use physical education curriculum activities to help each student develop control in gross and fine motor skills; to develop health-related fitness levels and skills for games, which give a sense of accomplishment and self-reliance (This is called functional movement.)

- To use childrens' natural impulses of running, skipping, jumping, etc., and lead them into an awareness of mastery of body movement in a personal, creative expression or dance form (This is called expressive movement.)

- To encourage movement exploration

- To develop social understanding through movement activities

- To provide kinesthetic reinforcement of concepts presented in the classroom (for example, to feel height, width, and length through jumping activities before measuring)

- To provide a medium for children to engage in movement activities that will develop kinesthetic awareness and lifelong motor skills

- To provide, in a controlled opportunity, sensory experiences that allow a systematic approach for the regulation of the central nervous system

The Environment

- The classroom, gymnasium, or outdoor facility—wherever students will meet—must allow the learner to have freedom of movement without fear or hindrance. Alter the size of the space based on the movement experiences you have planned as well as on the ability levels of students.

- Classrooms must be free of physical distractions if movement programs are to be conducted there. In addition, moving furniture and obstacles out of the way within the classroom provides a safe environment for children to move with confidence. Use creativity and flexibility to design a safe, inviting environment in which students may move freely.

- Gymnasium and outdoor facilities may also need to be modified to meet the needs of the students. Establish the boundaries of a larger environment or divide it to allow students a sense of space. Create these smaller spaces for movement within a large area by using cones or markers.

Suggested Methods and Procedures for Teaching a Specific Rhythmic Movement

A successful learning experience, in any activity, is dependent to a large extent upon the preparation of the teacher. Teachers are trained in overall methods of presenting materials in a given subject area. However, the variety of materials within a given area is often so great that it is necessary to give attention to specific procedures when preparing to teach a particular kind of material. For example, dance is an activity within a larger program of movement activities that requires attention to some rather specific suggestions for preparation. A teacher must be thoroughly familiar with the basic steps, music, and sequence of movement before attempting to teach the dance to students. Use the following guidelines to help prepare for a successful experience.

Teacher Preparation Includes:
- knowledge of the basic movements the dance or activity requires;
- understand the sequence of the movements and their relationship to the music;
- familiarity with the music, its introduction, sequence, and tempo;
- ability to demonstrate the movements accurately, with or without music;
- readiness of all of the needed materials in order to make the best possible use of class time;
- knowledge of the cognitive, motoric, and emotional characteristics of students; and
- preparation of a safe environment in which students may move freely.

Presentation of the Movement Activity

The analysis of a dance or movement activity, in order to teach it, will vary according to the movement activity and the ability levels of students. However, many of the steps in this procedure are similar and therefore are applicable to all types of dance and/or movement activities.

1. Give the name of the dance. Write it on the board.
2. Give facts and information about the dance or movement activity and share any background that will add interest and make the dance more meaningful. Such information need not be given all at once, but may be interspersed between movements when the dancers need a chance to rest.
3. Play a short part of the music to give the class an idea of the character, quality, and speed of the piece.
4. Arrange students in the desired formation. It may be practical to do this as a first step.
5. Teach the difficult movements or figures separately. Teach the parts independently of the whole. These sections should be mastered before the entire movement sequence is put together.
6. Talk through a movement without demonstrating it; then, demonstrate the movement without talking; then, direct the class in the pattern while talking and demonstrating at the same time.
7. For dances or movement activities with short sequences, demonstrate the entire movement activity and cue the class as they learn to do it. For dances or movement activities with long sequences, analyze a part, try it without the music first, and then move with the music. Continue learning one part at a time for the entire activity.
8. Give a starting signal. "Ready (pause) and" is a useful signal to help everyone begin together. Accent the word and. The first movement of the activity comes on the first accented beat after the word and. For students who are hard of hearing or deaf, use a hand signal. Practice giving the hand signal at the correct starting time.
9. If a partner is needed for the activity, choose a student to help demonstrate each part as it is explained to the group. As the new vocabulary words and the movements of the dance are explained, the partner should be able to follow along.
10. Correct errors in the whole group first and give individual help as it is needed later.
11. If possible, begin with the music at a slower tempo and gradually speed it up to the correct tempo. When using equipment without the ability to slow the tempo, teach the dance steps without music. Then, gradually speed up the steps, until the movement is the same tempo as the music.
12. Use the blackboard to help clarify movement patterns. Have the group clap difficult tempos and rhythms.
13. Cue the movement patterns until students have had sufficient practice to remember the routines without a signal.
14. Change plans if a movement activity proves too difficult or a poor choice for the group. Select another dance rather than spending time on a poor choice.
15. Be generous with praise and encouragement for the group.
16. Show personal enthusiasm and enjoyment for the dance or movement activity. A teacher's enthusiasm and genuine interest in what is being taught does much to help others enjoy it.

Review

1. Review the dance orally, having students tell the sequence of movement if possible. Then, try performing the dance movements with the music, cueing the important changes.
2. Pick out the spots that need review and practice them. Point out the details of the movement patterns. Repeat the movement activity.
3. Announce the dance several days later, play the music, and see how far the students can progress without a cue.
4. Avoid letting the class form the habit of depending on a cue to prompt them. Cueing should be used only as a teaching device.

Suggested Methods for Class Procedures

The suggestions that follow constitute rather specific guidelines for selecting materials, achieving variety within a class period, and using enrichment resources to make the class period a warm, friendly, and informative experience.

1. Materials should correspond to the skill level of the group.

2. Beginning activities should include the entire group. However, lower functioning groups may use only one or two activities at a time. Nonpartner circle dances are useful for this purpose.

3. The first movement activities should be simple and short.

4. Materials should be planned in progressive sequences so that each successive part learned is relevant to and dependent upon the preceding part.

5. Plan activities that make use of uneven numbers of boys and girls.

6. Plans should include frequent partner changes.

7. Allow time and opportunity for students to practice social responsibilities.

8. New steps and movement patterns should be practiced in the normal dance situation soon after they are introduced.

9. Include both new and review material in each lesson.

10. Arrange the movement selections in a lesson to provide for periods of activity and rest; contrast in style, step, and pattern; and variety in formation, such as circles, lines, sets, partners, etc.

11. Presentation of the material should include stimulating students' interest about the dances, for example, by sharing applicable cultural information. This gives some meaning to the dance and fosters greater appreciation of the style.

12. Discuss the unique features of a dance or movement activity to assist students in distinguishing one dance from another.

13. Allow ample time for practice, questions, requests, and suggestions. This is also the time to give valuable individual assistance.

14. Encourage original work. The social dancer is particularly eager to be free from set routines. In other dance forms, dancers may enjoy putting together their own routines for a variety of rhythmic patterns.

15. Supplement teaching with visual aides. Pictures, diagrams, maps, cartoons, articles, movies, and special demonstrations stimulate interest. These encourage students to try to solve the problem without imitating their neighbors. When working with a lower functioning group, the teacher's movements may serve as a visual cue for students to imitate.

16. Observe students' movement patterns and encourage them to use their own creative ideas.

17. Within a movement piece that stimulates the expression of free movement, facilitate the process by not directing student movements.

18. Allow students to copy and mirror the freedom of movement that other students demonstrate.

19. Provide an environment in which freedom of expression is encouraged and a "no right or wrong" atmosphere is present.

20. Whenever possible, connect the movement experiences to related educational outcomes in the academic setting.

Simple Movement Exploration Activities

The following activities are not organized by progression. These are simply suggestions for teachers to use as they assist students in exploring movement activities. Engaging in these actions will help students learn how their bodies work and develop a sense of body image. These ideas will enhance and facilitate students' abilities to move their bodies freely as they perform the dance and movement activities.

When creating your own movement activities for students, use three simple movement elements—speed, space, and force—to form your base of ideas and expand from there. Finally, be sure to incorporate students' suggestions as a basis for further problem solving.

1. Do something big and cover as much space as possible.
2. Do something big, covering as much space as possible, while moving in a straight line.
3. Be very low but take up as much space as possible.
4. Be very small and move in a straight line; then, move in a crooked line.
5. Do something tall and cover as much space in the air as possible while covering as little of the floor as possible.
6. Be low and cover as much floor space as you can.
7. Be high and cover all of the space you can.
8. Find a space by yourself. Be sure it is large enough to move around in without entering someone else's space. Move in your space any way you wish.
9. Do something upside down and small; then, move at the same time.
10. Do something upside down and big; then, move at the same time.
11. Be small and move fast; be small and move slowly.
12. Be big and move fast; be big and move slowly.
13. Start small; grow to be big and move with different speeds.
14. Start big; shrink to be small and move with different speeds.
15. Balance on one part of your body; balance on two parts; balance on three parts; etc.
16. Walk (run, skip, gallop, slide, etc.) in different directions around the floor. Then, change how you walk: Walk high. Walk low. Walk fast. Walk slowly. Walk heavily—stomp. Walk lightly—tiptoe.
17. Send your body into the air. Land softly; land heavily.
18. Make different shapes with your body while standing on two feet; make different shapes while in the air.
19. Move suddenly to another spot on the floor.
20. Collapse onto the floor.
21. Run, fall, and roll over; get up. Repeat over and over.
22. While in one place on the floor, stretch any part of your body; then, stretch all of the parts of your body.
23. Do a twisting movement in slow motion; then, do it very quickly. Twist with just a little effort; then, twist with a lot of effort.
24. Do a slow motion twist and then a stretch; repeat over and over.
25. Roll into as small a position as you can; stretch into as long a position as you can.
26. Think about different body parts; do a twist with as many different parts as you can.
27. Move very lightly around the floor; in one place; and with different parts of your body.
28. Move very forcefully around the floor; in one place; and with different parts of your body.
29. Turn slowly in circles as you move around the floor.
30. Find a friend. Together, make a letter or letters of the alphabet.

Vocabulary

Here is a natural opportunity for students to learn new words and new meanings of familiar words as they apply them to movement experiences. The proprioceptive information received through movement experiences provides a concrete sensory experience. This neural connection between the brain and the muscles and joints can assist in the development of receptive language skills.

When students move their bodies and explore creative movements, language and vocabulary development will be enhanced. During free movement activities, action words such as *crawl, dodge, flex, lunge,* etc., can be learned by connecting the physical act to the meaning of the word. As you lead these movement activities, facilitate this ongoing process of language acquisition.

A: above, abruptly, acrobatic, across, act, active, alarm, alive, angry, arch, around, arrow, aside, asleep, atop, attack, awake

B: back, back bend, back up, backward, balance, balk, ball, bam, bang, bark, barnstorm, barrel, bat, beat, bellow, bend, big, billow, blast, block, bloom, blow, bob, bobble, bolt, bomb, boom, boomerang, boot, bop, bore, bounce, bound, bow, bowl, box, brake, break, breezy, brush, bubble, bubbly, bump, burr, burst, buzz, by

C: carry, cartwheel, cast, catch, chain, chase, chug, circle, clang, clap, clasp, clench, click, climb, cling, clod, closer, close to, cloud, clown, coil, collapse, collide, conk, crack, crackle, crash, crawl, creep, cringe, crooked, cross, crumble, crunchy, cuddle, curl, curve, cutting

D: dance, dangle, dart, dash, deep, descend, die, dig, disappear, discover, disintegrate, dive, dodge, doodle, double up, down, drag, dream, dress, drift, drive, drop, duck, dump

E: easy, elevate, escape, evaporate, even, examine, exercise, explode

F: fade, fall, fall apart, fan, far, fast, fat, fearful, feather, fiddle, fight, find, fizzle, flat, flatten, flee, fleet, flex, flick, fling, flip, flit, float, flop, flow, flutter, fly, fold, form, forward, freeze, frown, furious

G: gallop, gaze, giant step, gigantic, glad, glare, glide, gnarl, go, gong, grab, grand, grapple, grasp, great, grimace, grind, grip, grow, growl, grumble, gurgle, gush

H: halt, hammer, hang, happy, hard, hasty, haul, heave, heavy, help, hide, high, hike, hip, hit, ho, hobble, hoe, holler, hook, hop, howl, hug, huge, hump, hunt, hurdle, hurry, hurt, husky

I: icy, idle, immobile, in, inch, inside

J: jab, jangle, jar, jerk, jet, jiggle, jitter, jog, jolly, jolt, jumble, jumbo, jump

K: kick, kneel, knock

L: lam, land, large, lash, laugh, launch, lazy, lean, leap, lift, light, lightning, limp, listen, little, lively, look, loop, loosely, loud, low, lug, lumber, lump, lunch, lunge

M: mad, malt, march, mash, melt, merry, motionless, mount, move, muddy, mush

N: near, nearby, nimble, nod

O: oh, on, on top of, open, ouch, out, over, overhead, ow

P: pant, pass, passive, pedal, pierce, ping, pitch, pitter-patter, plunge, plunk, poof, pop, pound, pour, power, prance, press, pretzel, probe, prowl, puff, pull, pump, punch, push, put

Q: quick, quickly, quiet, quit, quiver

R: race, racehorse, rag doll, rake, rap, rattle, reach, reel, relax, repeat, rest, restless, retrace, reverse, revolve, ride, rigid, ring, rip, rising, roar, rock, rocket, roll, romp, round, row, rubber, rumble, run

S: sad, sail, saw, scamper, scared, scat, scatter, scoot, scramble, scratch, scream, screech, scrunch, scurry, search, see, settle, shake, shift, shirk, shiver, shoot, shout, shudder, shuffle, shriek, shrill, shrink, shrivel, shrug, shush, sidestep, sideways, sigh, sink, sit, sizzle, skate, skid, skim, skip, slam, slap, slash, sleep, sleepy, slide, sling, slink, slip, slither, slop, slosh, slow, slug, slump, smack, small, smash, smile, smooth, snap, snappy, snarl, snatch, sneak, soar, soft, somersault, sour, spar, spin, spiral, splash, split, sprawl, sprightly, spring, sprint, spry, squash, squat, squeak, squeeze, squiggle, squirm, squish, stagger, stagnant, stalk, stamp, stand, step, stiff, still, sting, stomp, stoop, stop, storm, strain, stretch, strike, stroke, stroll, strong, strut, stumble, stunt, surge, swat, sway, sweep, swerve, swift, swim, swing, swipe, swirl, swish, swivel, swoop

T: tack, tackle, tag, tall, tangle, tap, tear, throw, thump, thunder, tick, tickle, tie, tightly, tilt, tingle, tinkle, tiny, tip, tiptoe, toddle, toes, topple, touch, tow, tower, tramp, travel, tread, tremble, trip, trot, tug, tumble, turn, turn over, twinkle, twirl, twist, twitch, twitter

U: uncurl, under, underneath, uneven, untie, up, upset, upside down

V: vanish, vast, vault, veer, vibrate

W: waddle, wail, wake-up, walk, wallop, waltz, wave, weak, weave, whack, whee, wheel, whip, whirl, whisper, whiz, whoa, whoop, whoosh, wide, widen, wiggle, wilt, wind, wing, wobble, wow, wrap, wrench, wrestle, wring, wrinkle

Y: yank, yell

Z: zigzag, zing, zip, zippy, zoom

Chapter 5: Stop and Go Games

Stop and go activities provide numerous benefits including the opportunity to develop and practice a variety of necessary skills. Participating in a stop and go game requires students to listen, follow a direction, and perform to the best of their abilities. In addition, the ability to stop when the music stops employs the same attention and concentration skills students need in the classroom. Stop and go activities also emphasize the important concept of closure—that an activity has a beginning and an end.

Stop and go activities can be used in any curriculum area. There are endless possibilities, so just use your imagination! Here is a sampling of some curriculum ideas that will strengthen both language arts and math skills:

Language Arts	Math
Picture Identification	Number Identification
Color Identification	Counting
Shape Identification	Ordinal Numbers
Letter Identification	Odd/Even Number Identification
Body Shape Letters	Sets
Letter Sounds Identification	Patterns
Blended Sounds	Heavy/Light
Upper- and Lowercase Letters	Greater Than/Less Than
Rhyming Words	Number Sentences
Spelling Words	What's Missing in Number Sentences
Compound Words	Addition/Subtraction
Word Sentences	Coin Recognition
Vowel/Consonant Identification	Money Recognition
Syllables	Telling Time
Synonym/Antonym Identification	Multiplication/Division
Noun/Verb Identification	Estimation
Days of the Week	Library Number System
Calendar	Zip Codes
Street Signs	

Gross Motor and Movement Stop and Go Games

Stop and Go

Equipment: CD or tape and player

Task Analysis: motor planning, muscular strength and endurance, cardiorespiratory endurance, bilateral activities, dynamic balance, body part awareness, locomotor skills, auditory memory, position in space, spatial relationships, figure-ground discrimination, lateralization, visual motor integration, attention and concentration, hypotonic

Description: Have students spread out through the play space. Select a piece of instrumental music with a beat that encourages movement (e.g., marching, dancing). Give students a direction, such as "Show me how you can roll like a log," and begin to play the music. Whenever you stop the music, students must stop, freezing in position, and wait for the next direction. Continue until all of the desired locomotor movements and/or animal walks have been performed.

Stop and Go Exercises

Equipment: cards, each with a number and an exercise word written on it (e.g., 10 jumping jacks) or a spinner (pattern found on page 63) with a number and an exercise word in each section; CD or tape and player

Task Analysis: motor planning, muscular strength and endurance, cardiorespiratory endurance, bilateral activities, dynamic balance, body part awareness, locomotor skills, auditory memory, position in space, spatial relationships, figure-ground discrimination, lateralization, form constancy, visual motor coordination, visual motor integration, attention and concentration, hypotonic

Description: Have students spread out through the play space. Select a piece of instrumental music with a beat that encourages movement. Give students a direction, such as "Show me how you can slide," and begin to play the music. Whenever you stop the music, hold up a card labeled with a number and exercise word. Students must perform the exercise the designated number of times. When all students have done the exercise, select the next movement to perform and begin the music again. Continue until all of the desired exercises have been performed.

Stop and Go Follow the Leader

Equipment: CD or tape and player

Task Analysis: motor planning, muscular strength and endurance, cardiorespiratory endurance, bilateral activities, dynamic balance, body part awareness, locomotor skills, auditory memory, position in space, spatial relationships, figure-ground discrimination, lateralization, form constancy, visual motor coordination, visual motor integration, attention and concentration, visual memory

Description: Have students spread out through the play space. Tell students to choose partners and then decide who in the pair will be the leader and who will be the follower. Select a piece of instrumental music with a beat that encourages movement. When the music begins to play, the leader will move around the play space using any type of movement and changing movements at any time. The follower will imitate the leader's movements. When you stop the music, tell students to switch places with their partners. Begin the music again with the new leaders and followers. Then, have students choose new partners to play the game again.

Stop and Go Statues

Equipment: CD or tape and player

Task Analysis: motor planning, muscular strength and endurance, cardiorespiratory endurance, bilateral activities, dynamic balance, body part awareness, locomotor skills, auditory memory, position in space, spatial relationships, figure-ground discrimination, lateralization, form constancy, visual motor coordination, visual motor integration, attention and concentration, visual discrimination, crossing the midline

Description: Have students spread out through the play space. Select a piece of instrumental music with a beat that encourages movement. Give students a direction, such as "Show me how you can walk like an elephant," and begin to play the music. When you stop the music, strike a pose (e.g., placing both hands on the head) to create a statue. Students should observe and create the same statue. Then, select the next movement to perform and begin the music again. Use your imagination to create statues appropriate for the developmental level of students; for example, incorporate yoga positions into the activity. Continue until all of the desired statue positions have been created.

Early Learning Stop and Go Games

Stop and Go Auditory Discrimination

Equipment: lummi sticks made from 0.5" (1.27 cm) diameter dowels and 12" (30.48 cm) in length, CD or tape and player

Task Analysis: motor planning, muscular strength and endurance, cardiorespiratory endurance, bilateral activities, dynamic balance, body part awareness, locomotor skills, auditory memory, position in space, spatial relationships, figure-ground discrimination, lateralization, auditory discrimination, attention and concentration

Description: Give each student a pair of lummi sticks and have students spread out through the play space. Select a piece of instrumental music with a beat that encourages movement. Give students a direction, such as "Show me how you can slither like a snake," and begin to play the music. Whenever you stop the music, tap a rhythmic pattern with your lummi sticks. Students must listen carefully and tap the same pattern. Then, they wait for the next direction about the movement to perform when the music begins again. Continue until all of the desired rhythmic patterns have been played.

Stop and Go Colors

Equipment: laminated colorful cards in any shape, CD or tape and player

Task Analysis: motor planning, muscular strength and endurance, cardiorespiratory endurance, bilateral activities, dynamic balance, body part awareness, locomotor skills, auditory memory, position in space, spatial relationships, figure-ground discrimination, lateralization, visual motor integration, attention and concentration, color recognition, hypotonic

Description: Scatter numerous laminated colorful cards on the floor throughout the play space. Have students spread out through the area. Select a piece of instrumental music with a beat that encourages movement. Give students a direction, such as "Show me how you can crawl," and begin to play the music. Whenever you stop the music, call out a color (e.g., orange). Students must find a card in the selected color, touch it with their toes, and wait for the next direction about the movement to perform when the music begins again. Continue until all of the desired colors have been called out.

Stop and Go Nonverbal Expressions

Equipment: emotion cards (found on pages 137–140), CD or tape and player

Task Analysis: motor planning, muscular strength and endurance, cardiorespiratory endurance, bilateral activities, dynamic balance, body part awareness, locomotor skills, auditory memory, position in space, spatial relationships, figure-ground discrimination, lateralization, visual motor integration, attention and concentration, visual memory, hypotonic

Description: Have students spread out through the play space. Select a piece of instrumental music with a beat that encourages movement. Give students a direction, such as "Show me how you can walk like a bear" and begin to play the music. Whenever you stop the music, hold up an emotion card. Students must act out the feeling on the card without using words. When all students have had the opportunity to portray the feeling, select the next movement to perform and begin the music again. Continue until all of the desired emotion cards have been displayed.

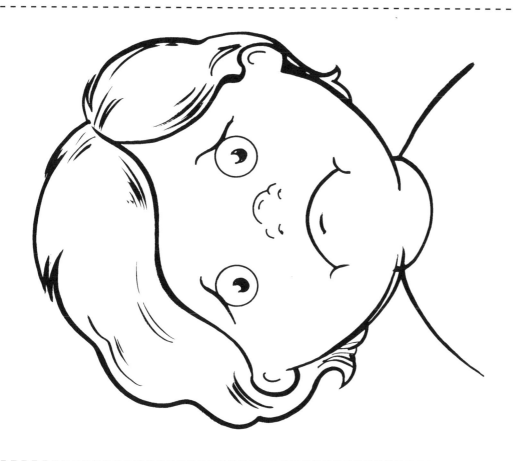

sad

happy

surprised

angry

scared

tired

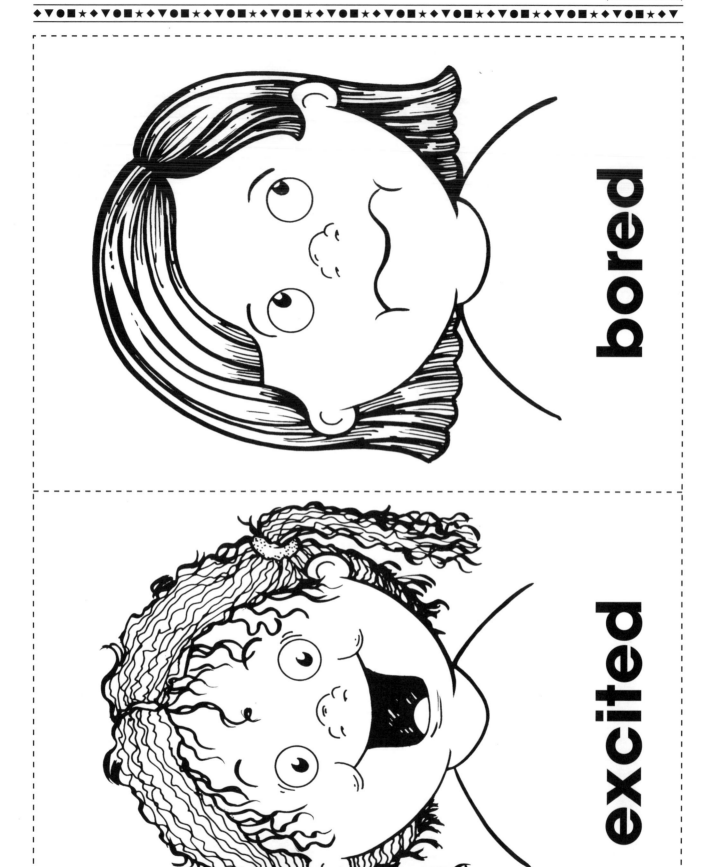

bored

excited

Stop and Go "Can You Touch . . . ?"

Equipment: CD or tape and player

Task Analysis: motor planning, muscular strength and endurance, cardiorespiratory endurance, bilateral activities, dynamic balance, body part awareness, locomotor skills, auditory memory, position in space, spatial relationships, figure-ground discrimination, lateralization, form constancy, visual motor coordination, visual motor integration, attention and concentration

Description: Have students spread out through the play space. Select a piece of instrumental music with a beat that encourages movement. Give students a direction, such as "Show me how you can tiptoe," and begin to play the music. Whenever you stop the music, ask a "Can you touch . . . ?" question (e.g., "Can you use your left elbow to touch something that is red and round?") Body part awareness and specific curriculum content, such as recognition of colors, shapes, words, and letters can all be included in this activity. Use your imagination. Students must look around the room to find objects to answer the question. When students have answered the question with their movements, select the next movement to perform and begin the music again.

Stop and Go Note Pitch

Equipment: keyboard or other tonal instrument (optional), CD or tape and player

Task Analysis: motor planning, muscular strength and endurance, cardiorespiratory endurance, bilateral activities, dynamic balance, body part awareness, locomotor skills, auditory memory, position in space, spatial relationships, figure-ground discrimination, lateralization, form constancy, visual motor coordination, visual motor integration, attention and concentration, visual discrimination, crossing the midline, auditory discrimination

Description: Have students spread out through the play space. Select a piece of instrumental music with a beat that encourages movement. Give students a direction, such as "Show me how you can bounce," and begin to play the music. When you stop the music, make either a high-pitched or a low-pitched sound. Students should listen carefully. If a high-pitched sound is heard, they should perform a high movement with their bodies. Conversely, if a low-pitched sound is heard, they should perform a low movement with their bodies. Then, select the next movement to perform and begin the music again. Continue until students have had several opportunities to demonstrate auditory discrimination.

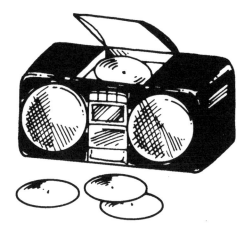

Stop and Go Animal Actions

Equipment: animal action cards (found on pages 142–145); CD or tape and player

Task Analysis: motor planning, muscular strength and endurance, cardiorespiratory endurance, bilateral activities, dynamic balance, body part awareness, locomotor skills, auditory memory, position in space, spatial relationships, figure-ground discrimination, lateralization, form constancy, attention and concentration

Description: Turn the animal action cards upside down and scatter them on the floor throughout the play space. Have students spread out through the area. Select a piece of instrumental music with a beat that encourages movement (e.g., marching, dancing, etc.). Give students a direction, such as "Show me how you can gallop," and begin to play the music. When you stop the music, choose the student who is closest to an animal card to turn the card over and read the animal's name aloud. All students will act out the animal's action. Then, select the next movement to perform and begin the music again. Continue until all of the animal cards have been read or all of the students have had a chance to read. Body part awareness and identification can also be included in this activity.

elephant

giraffe

monkey

horse

rabbit

cat

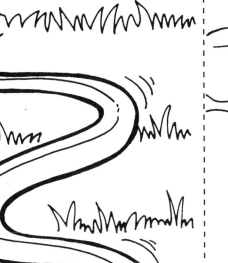

snake

fish

bird

turtle

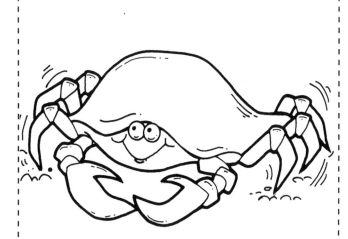

crab

gorilla

bull

squirrel

penguin

duck

Stop and Go Clothing Colors

Equipment: CD or tape and player

Task Analysis: motor planning, muscular strength and endurance, cardiorespiratory endurance, bilateral activities, dynamic balance, body part awareness, locomotor skills, auditory memory, position in space, spatial relationships, figure-ground discrimination, lateralization, form constancy, visual motor coordination, visual motor integration, attention and concentration, visual discrimination, crossing the midline, socialization

Description: Have students spread out through the play space. Select a piece of instrumental music with a beat that encourages movement. Give students a direction, such as "Show me how you can tiptoe," and begin to play the music. When you stop the music, call out a color. Students should look at their own clothing. If a student is wearing the chosen color, she remains standing. Students not wearing the color should squat down. Then, select the next movement to perform and begin the music again. Continue until all of the desired colors have been chosen or until no students are still standing.

Stop and Go Clue

Equipment: CD or tape and player

Task Analysis: motor planning, muscular strength and endurance, cardiorespiratory endurance, bilateral activities, dynamic balance, body part awareness, locomotor skills, auditory memory, position in space, spatial relationships, figure-ground discrimination, lateralization, form constancy, visual motor coordination, visual motor integration, attention and concentration, visual discrimination, crossing the midline, auditory discrimination

Description: Have students spread out through the play space. Select a piece of instrumental music with a beat that encourages movement (e.g., marching, dancing, etc.). Give students a direction, such as "Show me how you can walk like a bear," and begin to play the music. When you stop the music, give one clue that describes one of the students. Give students one chance to identify the chosen student from the given clue. Then, select the next movement to perform and begin the music again. Repeat, giving one clue at a time and one chance to guess who the chosen student is, and continue until the identity of the student has been revealed.

Stop and Go Following Directions

Equipment: following directions cards (found on pages 147–149); CD or tape and player

Task Analysis: motor planning, muscular strength and endurance, cardiorespiratory endurance, bilateral activities, dynamic balance, body part awareness, locomotor skills, auditory memory, position in space, spatial relationships, figure-ground discrimination, lateralization, form constancy, visual motor coordination, visual motor integration, attention and concentration, visual discrimination, crossing the midline, auditory discrimination

| March around in a circle. |
| Walk 4 steps on tiptoes. |
| Take 3 leaps forward. |
| Skip 6 steps forward. |

Description: Turn the directions cards upside down and scatter them on the floor throughout the play space. Have students spread out through the play area. Select a piece of instrumental music with a beat that encourages movement. Give students a direction, such as "Show me how you can leap," and begin to play the music. When you stop the music, choose three students to select and read out loud a directions card. Students must listen, process, and move according to the directions in the correct order. When all students have followed the directions correctly, select the next movement to perform and begin the music again.

Take 2 steps backward.

Take 3 leaps forward.

March around in a circle.

Hop 2 times.

Take 1 step sideways.

Walk 4 steps on tiptoes.

Hop once on the left foot.

Hop once on the right foot.

Take 2 small steps forward.

Take 3 giant steps forward.

Turn around 3 times.

Crab walk 4 steps forward.

Skip 6 steps forward.

Crawl backward 2 steps.

Take 2 leaps forward.

Flap arms and fly forward 5 steps.

Pounce forward 2 times.

Creep backward 3 times.

Stop and Go Bigger and Smaller

Equipment: a variety of objects in different sizes, CD or tape and player

Task Analysis: motor planning, muscular strength and endurance, cardiorespiratory endurance, bilateral activities, dynamic balance, body part awareness, locomotor skills, auditory memory, position in space, spatial relationships, figure-ground discrimination, lateralization, form constancy, visual motor coordination, visual motor integration, attention and concentration, visual discrimination, crossing the midline

Description: Have students spread out through the play space. Display an object. Select a piece of instrumental music with a beat that encourages movement. Give students a direction, such as "Show me how you can glide," and begin to play the music. When you stop the music, call out either "bigger" or "smaller." Students must find another object that is either bigger or smaller than the displayed object. When all students have chosen an object, display a new object, select the next movement to perform, and begin the music again. Continue until all of the desired objects have been displayed.

Stop and Go Positional Words

Equipment: positional word cards (found on pages 150–152), CD or tape and player

Task Analysis: motor planning, muscular strength and endurance, cardiorespiratory endurance, bilateral activities, dynamic balance, body part awareness, locomotor skills, auditory memory, position in space, spatial relationships, figure-ground discrimination, lateralization, form constancy, visual motor coordination, visual motor integration, attention and concentration, visual discrimination, crossing the midline

Description: Turn the positional phrase cards upside down and scatter them on the floor throughout the play space. Have students spread out through the play area. Tell students to choose partners and then decide who in the pair will be first to follow the direction. Select a piece of instrumental music with a beat that encourages movement. Give students a direction, such as "Show me how you can gallop," and begin to play the music. When the music stops, choose a student to turn over a card and read it. The first student in each pair will create the described position and then state it verbally. For example, "I am standing in front of my partner." Begin the music again with the partners switching places to follow the positional direction on the next card and create the described position. Then, have students choose new partners to play the game again. Continue until all of the desired positional words have been demonstrated.

(positional word cards)

out	**in**
on	**off**

under	over
in front	behind
next to	between
inside	outside
around	through
up	down

top	bottom
left	right
above	below
near	far
first	last
corner	beside

Language Arts Stop and Go Games

Stop and Go Letters

Equipment: letter cards (found on pages 33–41), CD or tape and player

Task Analysis: motor planning, muscular strength and endurance, cardiorespiratory endurance, bilateral activities, dynamic balance, body part awareness, locomotor skills, auditory memory, position in space, spatial relationships, figure-ground discrimination, lateralization, visual motor integration, attention and concentration, letter recognition, hypotonic

Description: Scatter numerous letter cards on the floor throughout the play space. Have students spread out through the area. Select a piece of instrumental music with a beat that encourages movement. Give students a direction, such as "Show me how you can skip," and begin to play the music. Whenever you stop the music, call out a letter. Students must find a card with the selected letter, touch it with their toes, and wait for the next direction about the movement to perform when the music begins again. Continue until all of the desired letters have been found.

Stop and Go Academic Ropes

Equipment: letter cards (found on pages 33–41), jump ropes, CD or tape and player

Task Analysis: motor planning, muscular strength and endurance, cardiorespiratory endurance, bilateral activities, dynamic balance, body part awareness, locomotor skills, auditory memory, position in space, spatial relationships, figure-ground discrimination, lateralization, visual motor integration, attention and concentration

Description: Give each student a jump rope and have students spread out through the play space. Select a piece of instrumental music with a beat that encourages movement. Direct students to begin jumping rope around the area when the music begins. Whenever you stop the music, hold up a letter card. Students must try to form the selected letter with their jump ropes on the floor. When all students have had the opportunity to form the selected letter with their ropes, begin the music again. Continue until all of the desired letters have been used.

Variation: Use word cards instead of letter cards. Students will work together in groups to form the words with their jump ropes.

Stop and Go Object Detectives

Equipment: CD or tape and player

Task Analysis: motor planning, muscular strength and endurance, cardiorespiratory endurance, bilateral activities, dynamic balance, body part awareness, locomotor skills, auditory memory, position in space, spatial relationships, figure-ground discrimination, lateralization, form constancy, visual motor coordination, visual motor integration, attention and concentration, visual discrimination, crossing the midline

Description: Have students spread out through the play space. Select a piece of instrumental music with a beat that encourages movement. Give students a direction, such as "Show me how you can shuffle," and begin to play the music. When you stop the music, describe an object that is visible to the students by giving descriptive hints. Students must listen carefully to the hints, find the object being described, and touch it. When all students have discovered the object, select the next movement to perform and begin the music again. Continue until all of the desired objects have been found.

Stop and Go Spelling

Equipment: letter cards (found on pages 33–41), cards with spelling words, CD or tape and player

Task Analysis: motor planning, muscular strength and endurance, cardiorespiratory endurance, bilateral activities, dynamic balance, body part awareness, locomotor skills, auditory memory, position in space, spatial relationships, figure-ground discrimination, lateralization, form constancy, visual motor coordination, visual motor integration, attention and concentration, visual discrimination, crossing the midline

Description: Scatter the letter cards throughout the play space and also give each student a letter to carry. Have students spread out through the area. Select a piece of instrumental music with a beat that encourages movement. Give students a direction, such as "Show me how you can scurry like a spider," and begin to play the music. When you stop the music, hold up a card with a spelling word. Students must find the letters—either by looking on the floor or working with other students and their letters—to correctly spell the chosen word. Increase the challenge by setting a time limit for students to spell the word. When students have correctly spelled the word, select the next movement to perform and begin the music again. Continue until students have spelled all of the desired words.

Stop and Go Rhymes

Equipment: rhyming word picture cards (found on pages 42–46), CD or tape and player

Task Analysis: motor planning, muscular strength and endurance, cardiorespiratory endurance, bilateral activities, dynamic balance, body part awareness, locomotor skills, auditory memory, position in space, spatial relationships, figure-ground discrimination, lateralization, form constancy, visual motor coordination, visual motor integration, attention and concentration, visual discrimination, crossing the midline, auditory discrimination

Description: Scatter the rhyming word picture cards throughout the play space and have students spread out through the area. Select a piece of instrumental music with a beat that encourages movement. Give students a direction, such as "Show me how you can slink like a panther," and begin to play the music. When you stop the music, hold up a picture card. Students must find another picture whose name rhymes with the chosen picture's name. Increase the challenge by setting a time limit for students to find a rhyming word picture. When students have found all of the rhyming word pictures, have them call out each word to identify the rhyme. Then, select the next movement to perform and begin the music again. Continue until students have found all of the desired rhyming word pictures.

Stop and Go Finish the Sentences

Equipment: narrative or short story, construction paper with "fill in the blank" sentences (each labeled with a student's name), crayons, CD or tape and player

Task Analysis: motor planning, muscular strength and endurance, cardiorespiratory endurance, bilateral activities, dynamic balance, body part awareness, locomotor skills, auditory memory, position in space, spatial relationships, figure-ground discrimination, lateralization, form constancy, visual motor coordination, visual motor integration, attention and concentration, visual discrimination, crossing the midline, graphomotor skills

Description: Scatter the pages of "fill in the blank" sentences throughout the play space and a place a crayon with each. Have students spread out through the area. Read the narrative or short story aloud. Select a piece of instrumental music with a beat that encourages movement. Give students a direction, such as "Show me how you can crawl," and begin to play the music. When you stop the music, each student should find the construction paper labeled with their name, read the first question, and answer it by filling in the blank. When all students have answered the first question, select the next movement to perform and begin the music again. Continue until students have answered all of the questions on their papers. At the end of the activity, have students meet as a group and share their answers.

Math Stop and Go Games

Stop and Go Numbers

Equipment: number cards (found on pages 53–56), cards with sets of dots, CD or tape and player

Task Analysis: motor planning, muscular strength and endurance, cardiorespiratory endurance, bilateral activities, dynamic balance, body part awareness, locomotor skills, auditory memory, position in space, spatial relationships, figure-ground discrimination, lateralization, visual motor integration, attention and concentration, number recognition, hypotonic

Description: Scatter numerous number cards on the floor throughout the play space. Have students spread out through the area. Select a piece of instrumental music with a beat that encourages movement (e.g., marching, dancing, etc.). Give students a direction, such as "Show me how you can jump on two feet," and begin to play the music. Whenever you stop the music, either call out a number, hold up a number card or a card with a set of dots to count. Students must find a card with the selected number, touch it with their toes, and wait for the next direction about the movement to perform when the music begins again. Continue until all of the desired numbers have been found.

Stop and Go Dominoes

Equipment: dominoes, number cards (found on pages 53–56), CD or tape and player

Task Analysis: motor planning, muscular strength and endurance, cardiorespiratory endurance, bilateral activities, dynamic balance, body part awareness, locomotor skills, auditory memory, position in space, spatial relationships, figure-ground discrimination, lateralization, visual motor integration, attention and concentration, number recognition, hypotonic

Description: Give each student a domino to hold and have students spread out through the play space. Select a piece of instrumental music with a beat that encourages movement. Give students a direction, such as "Show me how you can hop on one foot," and begin to play the music. Whenever you stop the music, hold up a number card (such as the number 8). Each student must find another student whose domino, when added to part of his domino, will equal the selected number (for example, 6 + 2 = 8). Students touch their dominoes *(See illustration, the girl's "2" domino section and the boy's "6" domino section equal "8")* then wait for the next direction about the movement to perform when the music begins again. Continue until all of the desired numbers cards have been displayed.

Variation: Use the activity to work on students' subtraction, multiplication, or division skills.

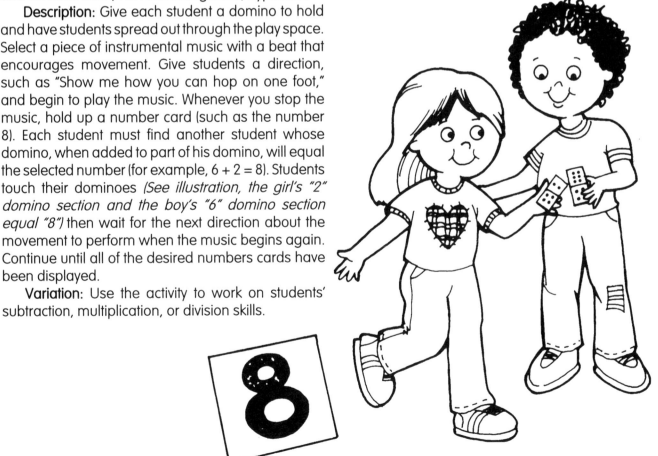

Chapter 6: More Curriculum and Movement Ideas

Silent Simon Says

Equipment: none

Task Analysis: motor planning, muscular strength and endurance, bilateral activities, static balance, body part awareness, position in space, spatial relationships, figure-ground discrimination, lateralization, form constancy, visual motor coordination, attention and concentration, visual discrimination, crossing the midline

Description: Have students sit on the floor facing you. In this activity, without talking, you will move your arms and/or hands to different body parts and/or positions in space (e.g., hands over the head). Begin by placing both hands, at the same time, to the knees (bilateral integration, symmetrical movements) and, without talking, wait for students to copy your actions. Then, move the hands to another body part (e.g., shoulders), wait again, and watch carefully to identify those students who are following and those who may have difficulty engaging in this activity.

Continue until students are following at the same pace. Based on the level of students, you might place one hand on the head and the other on a knee at the same time (bilateral integration, asymmetrical movements). The pace of the movement will also be determined by the developmental level of students. This activity is tremendous for developing visual motor integration, visual tracking, time on task, and attention and concentration. When children attain these skills, they will be better equipped for listening and following directions in a classroom.

Musical Simon Says

Equipment: CD or tape and player

Task Analysis: motor planning, muscular strength and endurance, bilateral activities, static balance, body part awareness, position in space, spatial relationships, figure-ground discrimination, lateralization, form constancy, visual motor coordination, attention and concentration, visual discrimination, crossing the midline

Description: Have students sit on the floor facing you. Select a piece of instrumental music that will encourage rhythmic movements. Without talking, move your arms and/or hands to different body parts on the beats of 8, 16, or 32. Begin by placing both hands at the same time to the knees (bilateral integration, symmetrical movements), tap the knees to the beat, and watch students as they follow and do the same. Continue by moving the hands to another body part (shoulders), continue to tap to the beat, and watch carefully for those students who are following and those who may have difficulty engaging in this activity.

Select the number of beats (8, 16, or 32) based on the developmental level of students (e.g., preschool students may need 16 or 32 beats to begin and stay on task, while older students can stay on task with only 8 beats). Using fewer beats will require more visual tracking and attention skill development as there will be more transitions during the musical piece. Using fewer beats should be the goal since this requires students to focus and attend throughout the activity. This activity is excellent for developing visual motor integration, visual tracking, time on task, and attention and concentration. When children attain these skills, they will be better equipped for listening and following directions in a classroom.

Vocabulary Words—Sign Language and Deaf Education

Equipment: pencils and paper

Task Analysis: motor planning, muscular strength and endurance, cardiorespiratory endurance, bilateral activities, dynamic balance, body part awareness, locomotor skills, auditory memory, position in space, spatial relationships, figure-ground discrimination, lateralization, form constancy, visual motor coordination, visual motor integration, attention and concentration, visual discrimination, crossing the midline, graphomotor skills

Yes

Thank You

Description: Teach students the letters of the sign language alphabet. After all of the letters have been learned, spell out a vocabulary word using sign language. The students will sign the word back and then write it down on the paper. In this activity, students must visually attend to the teacher, visually discriminate the movements of the fingers, and, in turn, spell out words using their fingers. Because this activity can stimulate the use of the fingers and thumb, it is a great activity for those students who are having difficulty holding a pencil with a static/dynamic tripod grip. Alternatively, instead of writing down the vocabulary word on paper, students can work in groups to spell out the word with their bodies, or find the word somewhere in the room and touch it with a selected body part.

Variation: Teach the children several words in sign language that can be used throughout the day. See the examples in the above illustrations.

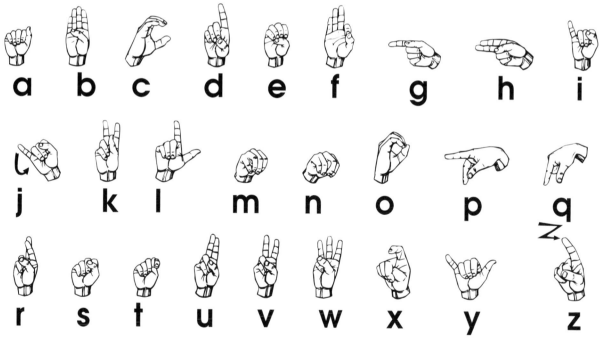

a b c d e f g h i

j k l m n o p q

r s t u v w x y z

Acting Out Action Words—Language Arts

Equipment: short story, play, or narrative that has action words

Task Analysis: motor planning, muscular strength and endurance, cardiorespiratory endurance, bilateral activities, dynamic balance, body part awareness, locomotor skills, auditory memory, position in space, spatial relationships, figure-ground discrimination, lateralization, form constancy, visual motor coordination, visual motor integration, attention and concentration, visual discrimination, crossing the midline

Description: Read a short story or narrative that includes many action words. Students can then retell the story by acting out the action words within small groups. By performing the action words, a student's body and mind connection becomes stimulated. Learning by doing is critical for primary age students.

Some Final Thoughts

With increasing pressure from federal legislation (No Child Left Behind), and local boards of education to raise test scores, educators have fallen into patterns of providing curriculum materials with less and less creativity and flexibility. What has been lost in this process is the understanding that the child develops not only cognitively (mind), but also motorically (body) and emotionally (spirit). The ability of the whole child to develop has been compromised due to the increased need to achieve higher test scores. In many classrooms today, we may only be educating children from the neck up. This practice needs to be revisited and closely examined.

Gross Motor Fun gives educators a chance to provide curriculum materials that meet the needs of the whole child. Engaging in movement develops cognitive, motoric, and emotional areas. Movement programs are vital, not only to the improvement of physical health and motor skill development, but also to the enhancement of self-esteem and self-confidence, thereby enriching the psychological well-being of students. As a result, these programs may enable students to perform more competently in classroom academics. In consideration of the cognitive, motoric, and emotional needs of the child, the perceptive teacher provides a success-oriented environment in which each child participates as fully as possible. *Gross Motor Fun* provides a "homerun" approach to meeting the needs of the whole child!

Children all learn differently. In the typical classroom, there are visual learners, auditory learners, tactile/physical learners, and emotional learners. Providing gross and fine motor opportunities for students to engage in as they learn has the potential to meet the needs of all of the students in the classroom.

In addition, when engaging the child with special needs, implementing these strategies in the classroom provides so many benefits. Special education law (IDEA) defines the least restrictive environment as the general education classroom where students with special needs can participate to the maximum extent as appropriate. As more and more students with special needs enter the general education classroom, there will be ongoing challenges to have them engage in the curriculum demands within the classroom. *Gross Motor Fun* offers teachers an opportunity to provide curriculum in a creative manner to better meet the unique needs of these students.

Engaging students in gross motor activities on a daily basis can also reduce inappropriate behavior. A feeling of accomplishment through movement activities enhances the self-esteem and self-image of all young children.

◆▼●■★◆▼●■★◆▼●■★◆▼●■★◆▼●■★◆▼●■★◆▼●■★◆▼●■★◆▼●■★◆▼●■★◆▼

Standard Correlations

This book supports the NCTE/IRA Standards for the English Language Arts, the recommended teaching practices outlined in the NAEYC/IRA position statement Learning to Read and Write: Developmentally Appropriate Practices for Young Children, the NCTM Principles and Standards for School Mathematics, and the National Association for Sport and Physical Education's National Standards for Physical Education.

―――――――――――――――― NCTE/IRA Standards for the English Language Arts ――――――――――――――――

Certain activities in this book support one or more of the following standards:
1. **Students read many different types of print and nonprint texts for a variety of purposes.** Students must read words, letters, or pictures for many of the games in *Gross Motor Fun*.
2. **Students use a variety of strategies to build meaning while reading.** Language arts activities in *Gross Motor Fun* focus on many skills including vocabulary, classification, letter and word identification, phonemic awareness, rhyming, sequencing, following directions, and spelling.
3. **Students communicate in spoken, written, and visual form, for a variety of purposes and a variety of audiences.** While doing the activities in *Gross Motor Fun*, students communicate both verbally and visually (through movement.)
4. **Students become participating members of a variety of literacy communities.** The group language arts games in *Gross Motor Fun* help teachers begin to build a literacy community.

―――― NAEYC/IRA Position Statement Learning to Read and Write: Developmentally Appropriate Practices for Young Children ――――

Certain activities in this book support one or more of the following recommended teaching practices for Preschool students:
1. **Adults create positive relationships with children by talking with them, modeling reading and writing, and building children's interest in reading and writing.** The many active language arts games in *Gross Motor Fun* help teachers build student interest in reading through movement.
2. **Teachers read to children daily, both as individuals and in small groups. They select high-quality, culturally diverse reading materials.** Several of the language arts activities in *Gross Motor Fun* begin with the teacher reading a passage aloud to her students.
3. **Teachers promote the development of phonemic awareness through appropriate songs, finger plays, games, poems, and stories.** *Gross Motor Fun* includes several phonemic awareness and rhyming games.
4. **Teachers provide opportunities for children to participate in literacy play, incorporating both reading and writing.** The fun and active literacy games in *Gross Motor Fun* engage students in reading through play.
5. **Teachers provide experiences and materials that help children expand their vocabularies.** The activities in *Gross Motor Fun* help build students' vocabularies in many areas, including the area of physical activity and movement.

Certain activities in this book support one or more of the following recommended teaching practices for Kindergarten and Primary students:
1. **Teachers read to children daily and provide opportunities for students to independently read both fiction and nonfiction texts.** Several of the language arts activities in *Gross Motor Fun* begin with the teacher reading a passage aloud to her students.
2. **Teachers provide opportunities for children to work in small groups.** Many of the games in *Gross Motor Fun* are played in small groups.
3. **Teachers provide challenging instruction that expands children's knowledge of their world and expands vocabulary.** The activities in *Gross Motor Fun* help build students' vocabularies in many areas, including the area of physical activity and movement.
4. **Teachers adapt teaching strategies based on the individual needs of a child.** Because many children learn kinesthetically, or through movement, the language arts games in *Gross Motor Fun* are a great way to adapt teaching to individual student needs.

―――――――――――――― This book supports the NCTM Principles and Standards for School Mathematics ――――――――――――――

This book and select activities in it support the following Number and Operations Standard Expectations for Grades Pre-K–2:
1. **Students count and recognize the number of objects in a set.** Many of the math games in *Gross Motor Fun* require students to count and recognize sets of objects.
2. **Students understand the relative position and size of ordinal and cardinal numbers.** Selected math games in *Gross Motor Fun* help students learn to compare and order numbers.
3. **Students understand and represent common fractions, such as 1/2, 1/3, and 1/4.** The "Cut Out The Fraction Relay" supports this standard.
4. **Students understand the meanings of addition and subtraction of whole numbers and how the two operations relate to each other.** *Gross Motor Fun* contains many addition and subtraction games that support this standard.
5. **Students understand what happens when they add or subtract whole numbers.** *Gross Motor Fun* contains many addition and subtraction games that support this standard.
6. **Students develop fluency in basic facts for addition and subtraction.** The addition and subtraction games in *Gross Motor Fun* help students become fluent in simple addition and subtraction.

7. **Students use different methods and tools to compute, including concrete objects, mental math, estimation, paper and pencil, and calculators.** The addition and subtraction games in *Gross Motor Fun* require students to compute using mental math.

This product and select activities in it support the following Algebra Standard Expectations for Grades Pre-K–2:
1. **Students sort, classify, and order objects by a variety of properties.** Several math games in *Gross Motor Fun* support this standard.
2. **Students recognize, describe, and extend simple sound, shape, or numeric patterns and change patterns from one form to another.** The "Clothespin Pattern Relay" game supports this standard.

This product and select activities in it support the following Geometry Standard Expectations for Grades Pre-K–2:
1. **Students identify, create, draw, compare, and sort two- and three-dimensional shapes.** Several games in *Gross Motor Fun* help students learn to identify shapes.
2. **Students describe, name, and interpret direction and distance and use ideas about direction and distance.** For many of the games in *Gross Motor Fun* that involve running, hopping, or tossing, students must use ideas about direction and distance.
3. **Students can interpret the relative position of objects.** The vocabulary taught in *Gross Motor Fun* includes positional concepts.

——————————— National Association for Sport and Physical Education National Standards for Physical Education ———————————

This book and the activities in it support the following Standards and Sample Performance Outcomes for K-2 Students:
A physically educated person:
Standard 1: Shows skill in movement skills and patterns needed for a variety of physical activities.
1. **Skips, hops, gallops, slides, etc. using proper form.** The tag, hopscotch, relay, and stop and go games in *Gross Motor Fun* support this standard.
2. **Performs simple dance steps in time with a particular tempo.** Activities in the "Creative Rhythms and Movement" chapter supports this standard.
3. **Shows the contrast between slow and fast movement when skipping, hopping, galloping, sliding, etc.** The simple movement explorations activities in the "Creative Rhythms and Movement" chapter support this standard.
4. **Can change directions quickly when traveling forward or sideways in a variety of ways.** The relay games in *Gross Motor Fun* support this standard.
5. **Makes smooth transitions between different kinds of movement in time to music.** The activities in the "Creative Rhythms and Movement" chapter support this standard.
6. **Taps a ball from foot to foot while standing in one place, shifting weight from foot to foot.** The Foot Dribbling Relay in *Gross Motor Fun* supports this standard.
7. **Drops a ball and catches it at the highest point of its bounce.** The Bounce and Catch Relay in *Gross Motor Fun* supports this standard.
8. **Throws a ball underhand using proper form.** The hopscotch games and various relay games in *Gross Motor Fun* support this standard.
9. **Balances on different body parts, like a statue.** Number Balance Tag, Stop and Go Statues, and various activities in the "Creative Rhythms and Movement" chapter support this standard.

Standard 2: Understands movement concepts, principles, strategies, and tactics as they apply to learning and doing physical activities.
1. **Correctly identifies body parts such as knee, foot, arm, palm, etc.** Several games in *Gross Motor Fun* specifically address knowing the parts of the body.

Standard 3: Regularly takes part in physical activity.
1. **Participates in moderate to vigorous physical activity on a regular basis.** All the games in *Gross Motor Fun* encourage moderate to vigorous physical activity.
2. **Takes part in a variety of physical activities that include the manipulation of objects (such as tossing a ball) both in and outside physical education class.** *Gross Motor Fun* includes many games that involve tossing objects such as balls or beanbags.

Standard 4: Attains and preserves a healthy level of physical fitness.
1. **Participates in a group of locomotor activities (including hopping, walking, jumping, galloping, and running) without getting tired easily.** The tag, relay, and stop-and-go games in *Gross Motor Fun* support this standard.
2. **Takes part in different games that increase breathing and heart rate.** Some games, in particular the tag and relay ones, in *Gross Motor Fun* can support this standard.

Standard 5: Shows self-respect and respect for others while participating in physical activity.
1. **Follows directions for all-class activities.** All the games in *Gross Motor Fun* support this standard.
2. **Works in a group setting without interfering with others.** All the games in *Gross Motor Fun* support this standard.
3. **Talks with a partner about how they are doing during practice.** The partner dance activities in the "Creative Rhythm and Movement" chapter support this standard.
4. **Enjoys exploring movement in tasks they do alone.** Activities in the "Creative Rhythm and Movement" chapter support this standard.